ANCIENT GREECE

A Comprehensive Resource
for the Active Study of Ancient Greece

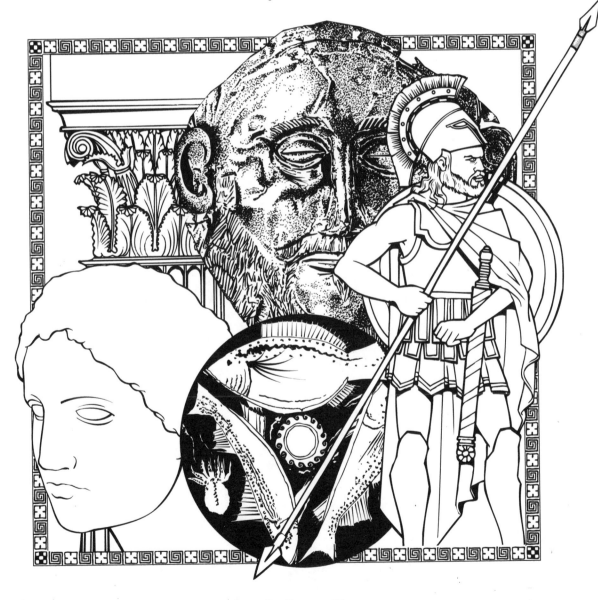

Written by George Moore

Published by World Teachers Press®

D1312199

Published with the permission of R.I.C. Publications Pty. Ltd.

Copyright © 2001 by Didax, Inc., Rowley, MA 01969. All rights reserved.

First published by R.I.C. Publications Pty. Ltd., Perth, Western Australia. Revised by Didax Educational Resources.

Printed in the United States of America.

Order Number 2-5176
ISBN 1-58324-110-8

D E F G H I 07 06 05 04 03

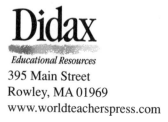

Educational Resources
395 Main Street
Rowley, MA 01969
www.worldteacherspress.com

ANCIENT GREECE

Foreword

For approximately 500 years from ca. (about) 800 B.C. to ca. 300 B.C., during the Archaic period and the Classical Age, the Greek city-states, particularly Athens, enjoyed one of the most interesting periods in the history of the world. It was a civilization which has inspired scholars who have studied the ancient Greeks. They call part of this period the Golden Age.

These years saw the introduction of the Phoenician alphabet to the Greek world, an alphabet which developed into Greek script and meant Homer's two literary masterpieces, the "Iliad" and the "Odyssey," could be recorded for future historians.

Dozens of small city-states were scattered around the country and their size and independence meant the people felt their opinions mattered. This probably encouraged the development of the world's first democracy in Athens around 500 B.C., despite some city-states being ruled by tyrants from around 650 B.C.

When Greece became part of the Roman Empire around 146 B.C., the more cultured and educated Greeks taught the Romans new building methods, painting styles, mathematics, writing and even how to organize the running of the Empire.

The influence of the advances made by the ancient Greeks in philosophy, the sciences, the arts and architecture is still felt today. The concept of democracy where ordinary people had their say and so were involved in the running of their towns centuries ago, is the basis of many democratic governments in our modern world.

"Hellas" was the name of the Greek world in ancient times. The word "Greek" came from the Roman name for them—Graeci.

Contents

TEACHER'S NOTES

Ancient Greece provides you with an in-depth review of this ancient civilization, presented through text, pictorial representation and a wide range of written and oral activities.

Written Activities

Activities include a wide range of learning areas and strategies. The presentation of informational text provides ideal opportunity for use within a language program, while the content is suited to studies of society and history. This mix is an ideal resource to promote cross-curricula learning. Activity types include:

- comprehension
- cloze
- arts and crafts
- literature study
- mapping
- puzzles
- sequencing
- matching
- debating

Oral Activities

The story of Ancient Greece is a fascinating one that provides ideal motivation for small group and whole class discussion. Many opportunities are identified throughout this book for discussion to occur on the different aspects of life in ancient times. These discussions are ideally done in a comparative model with the students daily life. Use of the other two books in this series, *Ancient Egypt* and *Ancient Rome* also provide opportunities for comparative discussions and studies.

Teacher's Notes

Teacher's Notes are provided for each activity. This includes detailed information that provides you with a greater level of background in order to promote and assist discussion on the topic. These pages are also presented in a manner where the student can use the page as additional information and further activities can be developed on this text.

At the bottom of this page, additional activities are suggested where appropriate.

Activity Pages

Provide detailed information on the aspect of Ancient Greece being studied. This text is provided in sufficient detail for discussion to occur in small or whole class groups. Each passage of text/information is accompanied by an activity as outlined above.

TEACHER'S NOTES

HEALTH

Teacher's Notes

Hippocrates taught that "every disease has its own nature, and arises from external causes", and that diseases were not a punishment handed down by the gods. He realized open wounds could become infected but didn't know why. He also believed the body had natural defenses to fight disease, something we now know to be true. His writings introduced the concept of preventing sickness through diet and life-style, and he suggested that the weather and drinking water could affect the health of the citizens. "Nature of Man" by Hippocrates describes how illnesses were caused by an imbalance of liquids in the body, a reason why later Greek doctors sometimes drew blood from patients' arms for they believed blood contained disease.

Public health physicians working for the State had to announce their qualifications at the "ekklesia", the people's assembly.

One herb, hyssop, used for coughs and chest infections, was still in use in the 20th century.

In the third century B.C. the physician Herophilus was interested in the medicinal qualities of new drugs and also developed a diagnostic method using different pulse beats. Even after ancient Greece was conquered by the Romans, the Greeks were regarded as the most important teachers of medical knowledge.

Sick people often made terra-cotta or bronze models to show physicians or priests which part of the body was affected. Models of ears, noses, breasts, legs and eyes have been unearthed in archaeological excavations, especially those which uncovered ancient shrines.

Additional Activity
Many doctors around the world swear a modern version of the Hippocratic Oath before they practice their profession. Find the modern version and discuss any differences.

Teacher's Notes

Additional information provided for teacher can also be used by students for additional information and activity.

Suggested Activity

Include a variety of activities to be used for further development of the topic.

Topic Text

Text and illustrations provide a solid base of information on the topic being studied.

Activity

A wide variety of activities are provided to develop the study of the topic.

HEALTH

Though the ancient Greeks had a god of medicine, Asclepius, they were the first people to separate medical treatment from methods which used religion, myth and witchcraft. This happened around 400 BC when the teachings of Hippocrates were generally accepted by physicians. Hippocrates was the son of a physician and was born and practiced on the island of Kos, though he also appears to have traveled widely spreading his beliefs.

Hippocratic bench

Broken bones were pulled into place and then splints used to help them to set.

We refer to Hippocrates as the "father of medicine". He studied his patient's symptoms before making a diagnosis and made notes on the effects of different medicines, thus treating medicine more scientifically. His Hippocratic Oath, associated with his teachings but probably not written by him, described the moral standards for doctors and has helped physicians, then and now, to enjoy a respected place in society.

There were many private doctors in Greece but Athens also had a public health service with doctors chosen and paid by the State. Doctors performed operations with simple instruments made from bronze, but since there were no anesthetics, they were painful and patients often died from infection or shock. Dentists used fillings of gold or even lead, they weren't aware of lead's poisonous properties. Sick people often made sacrifices at a temple and then slept there overnight, hoping to be cured by the next morning. Temple priests were Greece's earliest doctors and they treated diseases with a mixture of herbs, diets, magic, exercise or rest.

Excavated metal surgical instruments.

Many poor children suffered from diseases like rickets through lack of vitamins, and the doubtful qualities of drinking water led to many stomach complaints. Ancient Greek doctors, of course, had no solution for disease epidemics and a plague caused by flea-ridden rats in Athens around 430 B.C. killed thousands, including the great statesman Pericles.

Activity Box
Use the given words to complete part of one translation of the Hippocratic code of conduct.

goact	give	asked	secret	benefit	females	divulge	corruption	professional
allmen	hear	slaves	houses	counsel	abstain	medicine	connection	

"I will _____[1] no deadly _____[2] to anyone if _____[3], nor

suggest any such _____[4]; … Into whatever _____[5] I enter, I will

_____[6] into them for the _____[7] of the sick, and will _____[8] from

every voluntary _____[9] of mischief and _____[10]; and further from the seduction of

_____[11] or males, of freemen and _____[12]. … Whatever, in connection with my

_____[13] practice or not in _____[14] with it, I see or _____[15], in the

life of _____[16], which ought not to be spoken of abroad, I will not _____[17], as

reckoning that _____[18] such should be kept _____[19]."

THE EARLY GREEKS

Teacher's Notes

Around 1200 B.C., the importance and power of the Mycenaean civilization declined. The use of stone for building was discontinued and Greece became a collection of villages. The art of writing was forgotten, but the early examples of Mycenaean writing on the Linear B clay tablets found in the excavations at Knossos were translated by modern scholars in the 1950s. The Mycenaeans copied letters from the Minoan Linear A script and then added letters of their own.

From around 1200 B.C., the next 400 years are known as the Dark Ages of Greece, when there was little trade. Then the Greek civilization began to flourish again and trade expanded as writing was rediscovered when an alphabet was borrowed from the Phoenicians. Around 800 B.C., the villages became towns with protective fortresses and defensive walls. Groups of towns evolved into the city-states like Athens and Sparta.

When the royal graves of Mycenaean chieftains were unearthed by Heinrich Schlieman in the 19th century, they were full of treasures—golden necklaces, the famous gold masks, jewelry and daggers inlaid with gold and silver.

The Mycenaean civilization didn't have much influence on later Greek life but they are generally recognized as the first Greeks, for the Minoan culture wasn't developed from Indo-European origins as was the case with mainland Greece. They learned new skills from the Minoans, who built splendid palaces at Knossos and could read and write. Around 1450 B.C., the more warlike Mycenaeans occupied Knossos and ruled Crete.

The Minoans were named after Minos, a legendary king.

Shaft grave from Mycenae

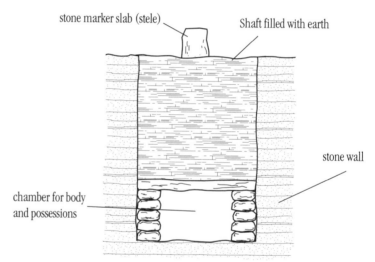

stone marker slab (stele)

Shaft filled with earth

stone wall

chamber for body and possessions

Gold mask from the royal tombs at Mycenae

The Dorian Greeks fought in chariots with weapons of iron, stronger than the bronze weapons of the southern Greeks. It is believed that they conquered most southern city-states, except Athens. Many Greeks hated the Dorians, so they migrated to the Greek islands and even traveled to Turkey, the site of ancient Troy.

Ancient Greece

www.worldteacherspress.com ©World Teachers Press®

THE EARLY GREEKS

The first important civilization in the Mediterranean Sea was the Minoan, centered at Knossos, on the island of Crete. The wealthy Minoans, who probably didn't speak Greek, traded with Syria, Egypt and the Greek mainland and the later Mycenaeans learned a lot from their culture.

The first prosperous ancient Greek civilization on the mainland was around 1500 B.C. and centered on the city of Mycenae. The original Mycenaeans were tribes of warlike, chariot-riding herdsmen who had swept down from northern Europe centuries before. In time, they built separate small kingdoms, traded with neighbors and developed a written language. Mycenae became the richest and most powerful city in Ancient Greece until around 1150 B.C. when the Mycenaean kingdoms were overrun by the Dorians, other invaders from northern Greece whose main city became Sparta.

The Dorians spoke a kind of Greek but knew nothing about reading and writing and the Greek civilization went into decline for several centuries.

Many areas of mainland Greece consisted of mountains and deep valleys. Over the centuries, city-states, large and small, developed but had little contact because of the terrain, except when involved in wars between cities, especially Athens and Sparta. There was no country called Greece (the ancient Greeks called it Hellas— "the place with a Greek way of life") but the inhabitants spoke Greek and each city-state controlled the land around it and made its own laws. As Athens, Sparta and other Greek cities like Corinth and Thebes grew larger and more important, Greek settlements began to develop in southern Italy and North Africa in cities like Alexandria, Cyrene and Syracuse, and Marseilles in France.

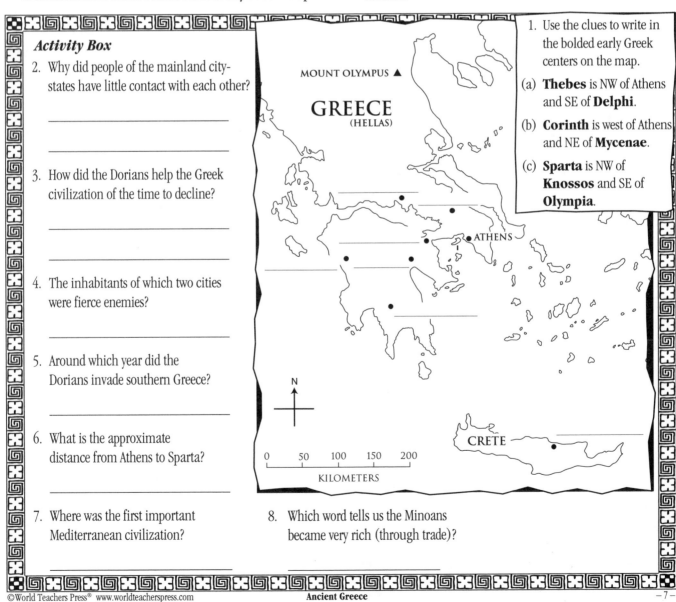

Activity Box

2. Why did people of the mainland city-states have little contact with each other?

    _____

    _____

3. How did the Dorians help the Greek civilization of the time to decline?

    _____

    _____

4. The inhabitants of which two cities were fierce enemies?

    _____

5. Around which year did the Dorians invade southern Greece?

    _____

6. What is the approximate distance from Athens to Sparta?

    _____

7. Where was the first important Mediterranean civilization?

    _____

1. Use the clues to write in the bolded early Greek centers on the map.

(a) **Thebes** is NW of Athens and SE of **Delphi**.

(b) **Corinth** is west of Athens and NE of **Mycenae**.

(c) **Sparta** is NW of **Knossos** and SE of **Olympia**.

MOUNT OLYMPUS ▲

GREECE
(HELLAS)

● ATHENS

N

0   50   100   150   200
KILOMETERS

CRETE

8. Which word tells us the Minoans became very rich (through trade)?

    _____

TIME LINE

Teacher's Notes

B.C.

1600   The early Mycenaeans built palaces on sites like Mycenae and small, rich kingdoms flourished.

1150   The Mycenaean age ends and a period of approximately 400 years known as the Dark Ages begins.

ca. 750   Homer's epic poems tell us about the siege of Troy and the travels of Mycenaean hero, Odysseus. Later excavations have shown that the legendary poem the "Iliad" has some basis in fact when it describes the Trojan war. However, historians believe there are inconsistencies—the Mycenaeans of those times buried their dead, whereas in Homer's poem the dead are cremated.

ca. 500   Cleisthenes, an Athenian statesman, introduces democratic political reforms which are lost at times in later periods when Athens is defeated by its enemies.

490   The Persians, under their leader Darius, invade Greece and attack Athens.

480   The Persian leader is Xerxes, son of Darius, the Persian ruler.

460–429   During the beginning of the period known as the Age of Pericles, the Parthenon is built on the Acropolis.

431   The Peloponnese is the large, wide peninsula joined to northern Greece by the isthmus of Corinth.

430   The plague lasts four years and about a quarter of the overcrowded population die, for many people have fled to Athens at the start of war with the invading Spartans.

371   The Theban general Epaminondas defeats the Spartans at the battle of Leuktra and Sparta's power is finally ended.

338   Philip's huge army defeats the Greeks who have to accept him as leader and forfeit their democratic way of life, but Athens remains the cultural center of Greece.

TIME LINE

Mycenaean octopus pot

Possible arrival of first Greek-speaking people from the north and east. — ca.* 2100 — B.C.

1600 — Mycenaean civilization begins.

Siege of Troy—believed to be the approximate date of the Trojan war. — ca. 1250

1150 — Dorians destroy Mycenaean kingdoms.

The city-state of Sparta founded. — ca. 900

ca. 776 — The first Olympic Games held at Olympia.

The poet Homer writes his epic poems the "Iliad" and the "Odyssey." — ca. 750

Homer

ca. 600 — First Greek coins made.

Birth of democracy in Athens. — ca. 500

490 — Persians defeated by Athenians at battle of Marathon.

Athens defeats the Persian fleet at the sea battle of Salamis. — 480

460 — The building of the long walls linking Athens with its port of Piraeus.

The democratic city-state of Athens flourishes under Pericles. — 460–29

431 — Sparta attacks Athens and the Peloponnesian War lasts 27 years.

A plague sweeps through Athens. — 430

379 — Thebes and Athens at war with Sparta.

Sparta defeated by a general from Thebes. — 371

359 — Philip II becomes king of Macedonia.

Philip defeats the Greeks at the battle of Chaeronea. — 338

336 — Philip is murdered and his son, Alexander the Great, becomes the king.

Alexander the Great

The Romans destroy Corinth, and Greece and Macedonia are ruled by Rome. — 146

*(ca. — about)

Activity Box

1. Athens surrenders to Sparta at the end of the Peloponnesian War in

   _____ B.C.

2. When did Greece become part of the Roman empire?

   _____ B.C.

3. Which city-state helped Athens in battles with Sparta?

   _____

4. How long did the Mycenaean kingdoms last?

   _____

5. Who lost the battle of Marathon?

   _____

6. Who was the father of Alexander the Great?

   _____

7. Who brought the Mycenaean age to an end?

   _____

8. How many decades were there between the battles of Salamis and Marathon?

   _____

9. Where were the Olympic Games first held?

   _____

10. Why do you think the Athenians built walls from Athens to Piraeus?

    _____

LANGUAGE (1)

Teacher's Notes

In 1936, Sir Arthur Evans gave lectures about the Mycenaean Linear B tablets he had excavated. He gave them that name, linear script, because many of the letters were carved with straight lines. Evans told his audience the language was unknown and no interpretation had been found. In the audience was Michael Ventris, a 14-year-old student. He was keen to solve the mystery and, after leaving the Air Force after World War II, he became an architect but spent years studying the script. Eventually he discovered they were records of stores, tax accounts and names of soldiers. No one has come up with a better interpretation.

The Greek alphabet spread around the shores of the Mediterranean and was adopted and modified by nations like Etruria. The Roman alphabet, the one we use today, was derived from a variation of the Greek alphabet used in the Greek colonies in southern Italy. Even the word "Greeks" is Latin as the Greeks called themselves "Hellenes," a word which described the different Aegean communities who believed they all belonged to one race.

Additional Activity

Create an alphabet of your own (perhaps 5 vowels, 10 consonants) and send a message to a partner.

For example:

        A could be ⋀

        F could be ⊤

        B could be ▷

LANGUAGE (1)

The Mycenaeans had used the Linear B script, which was then forgotten when their civilization went into decline after the Dorian invasions. After these Dark Ages (ca. 1200–800 B.C.), when writing skills disappeared, the Greeks began to trade with the Phoenicians, who lived in the eastern Mediterranean where Lebanon is today. Around 800 B.C., they borrowed letters from the Phoenician alphabet which had been used from around 1000 B.C. The Greeks added extra signs for vowels as the original Phoenician alphabet contained only consonants. The Phoenicians spoke the vowel sounds but did not write them down. In the Greek system, a single character (a grapheme) represents a single sound (a phoneme), e.g., the "p" in "put," "spin" and "top."

Around 500 B.C., the Greeks began to write from left to right after years of writing in both directions.

Greek writers wrote on paper made from papyrus from Egypt but very few of their rolls have survived. The Romans, admirers of Greek culture, made many copies of Greek writings when Greece became part of the Roman Empire and these have been a source of knowledge for scholars studying ancient Greece.

Early Greek alphabet 800 B.C.	Classical Greek alphabet 200 B.C.		Name of Greek letter	Modern alphabet
	Capital	Small letter		
◁	A	α	alpha	A
Γ	B	ß	beta	B
←		no C	→	C
◁	Δ	δ	delta	D
Ɛ	E	∈	epsilon "e" sound as in let	E
←		no F	→	F
Γ	Γ	γ	gamma	G
⊟	H	η	eta "e" sound as in day	H
∫	I	ι	iota	I
←		no J	→	J
K	K	κ	kappa	K
Γ	Λ	λ	lambda	L
Ϻ	M	μ	mu	M
Ν	N	ν	nu	N
O	O	o	omicron "o" sound as in hot	O
Γ	Π	π	pi	P
←		no Q	→	Q
P	P	ρ	rho	R
≶	Σ	σς	sigma	S
Τ	Τ	τ	tau	T
Y	Υ	∨	upsilon	U
←		no V,W	→	V,W
‡	=	ξ	xi	X
←		no Y	→	Y
None	Z	Ζ	zeta	Z
None	Θ	θ	theta	TH
None	Φ	φ	phi	PH
None	X	χ	chi	KH
None	Ψ	ψ	psi	PS
None	Ω	ω	omega "o" sound as in cold	O

LANGUAGE (2)

Teacher's Notes

See page 10 for Language background information and teacher's notes.

LANGUAGE (2)

Activity Box

1. Discuss with your partner any links you can see between our alphabet and an earlier one. List them below.

   _____

   _____

2. Where does the word "alphabet" come from? _____

   _____

3. Translate these words:

   (a) δЄαδ _____ (b) λαΜβ _____

   (c) ΚΡϝΑΔ _____ (d) ΚΟϝϝΡ _____

   (e) ΤΒΔΛΚϹ _____ (f) Υρατ _____

4. Make up some words for the other students to translate. Do not mix alphabets.

   (a) _____ (b) _____

   (c) _____ (d) _____

   (e) _____ (f) _____

5. Which letter shapes are the same in the three alphabets?

   _____

6. Which letter shapes are similar?

   _____

7. Write your name in each of the alphabets listed below.

   a. Early Greek

   _____

   b. Classical Greek

   _____

   c. Modern

   _____

GOVERNMENT (1)

At a funeral speech to honor the war dead, Pericles said Athens "does not try to copy the laws of our neighbors … because arrangements are not in the hands of the few but of the many, its name is Democracy."

Teacher's Notes Every citizen of Athens had the right to speak or vote at the Public Assembly (ekklesia). A citizen was a free man born to Athenian parents. The Assembly met on a hill in the city about 40 times each year and needed 6,000 citizens for a meeting to be held. Meetings began with the question, "Who wishes to speak to the Assembly?" and voting appears to have been by the use of pebbles or a show of hands. If the crowd was smaller than required, more citizens were rounded up by officials. Periclean Athens had a population of about 300,000.

The Athenian council met every day except holidays and unlucky days. Council members served for a year and could serve for a second term after being out of the Council for a time. The councilors met in a round building called the Tholos and there was always someone on duty day or night, in case of an emergency.

In the reforms introduced by Cleisthenes, the archons, or magistrates were selected by lot instead of election and they became less important. The only officials not chosen by lot were the commanders of the Athenian army and navy.

ca. 800–650 B.C. Most Greek city-states were run by rich landowners called aristocrats. This rule was by the privileged few—magistrates were elected each year from the nobility.

ca. 650–500 B.C. Dissatisfaction with the aristocrats led to the rule of tyrants in many states and the first tyrant seized power in Corinth in 650 B.C. It became the most common form of government in Ancient Greece for 150 years, though many were not cruel or oppressive. Only the city-states Sparta and Aegina were not ruled by tyrants.

Draco's laws were harsh and his name has given us our word "draconian." Under his system of laws, the stealing of a cabbage was punishable by death.

GOVERNMENT (1)

Pericles

Around 460 B.C., when Pericles ruled Athens, Sparta and Athens were the two most powerful city-states. Sparta was a military state which had defeated the people of Laconia and Messenia and made them slaves called "helots." Sparta was a kingdom whereas Athens, under Pericles, was moving once more towards a democratic state as it had been around 500 B.C. under the democratic reforms by the enlightened aristocrat Cleisthenes, one of the tyrants (sole rulers) of that period.

Cleisthenes divided the people of Attica (Athens and the surrounding region) into 10 tribes from three regions—the inland, the coast and the city. The tribes were then split into about 150 smaller communities, called "demes." Each tribe sent 50 representatives over the age of 30 to the Council. Councilors were chosen by lot and each tribe took turns to lead the Council. The Council drafted laws and proposals for running the State which then were debated in the Assembly.

Ancient Athens was possibly the only real democracy in the history of the world. Decisions were made by popular vote and there were no political parties or professional politicians.

Sparta was not as democratic. It was ruled by two kings, each representing a different tribe, and a Council of 28 aristocrats, each over 60 years of age. The Council sent matters to be discussed to the Assembly, made up of all citizens over 30 years of age.

Before 650 B.C. and the period of rule by tyrants (ca. 650–500 B.C.), Athens was ruled by a king with a council of aristocrats whose decisions were carried out by nine magistrates called "archons." Archons were elected annually and included three chief magistrates with special powers. The Athenians were disappointed with this system and laws were very strict—even minor crimes were punishable by death.

In our democracy, all enrolled citizens have the right to vote, but in ancient Greek "demokratia" only Athenian citizens had the franchise. Women, foreign residents in Athens ("metics") and slaves ("helots") were excluded.

Activity Box

1. Who ruled Athens around 460 B.C.?

    _____

2. Create a flow diagram to show how the people of Attica were represented by the council.

3. Explain why Athens is seen as the the only real democracy in the history of the world.

    _____

    _____

4. Explain how our current democracy is different to democracies of this time.

    _____

    _____

GOVERNMENT (2)

Teacher's Notes

See page 14 for Government background information and teacher's notes.

Ancient Greece

GOVERNMENT (2)

Across

2. Tribal region
6. Make a choice
7. Groups of people
9. Inhabitants
11. A nobleman
15. Small communities
16. Very old
19. Legal rule
21. Conquered by Sparta
22. Athens was a _____ state
23. Severe

Down

1. Sparta was one
3. An aristocrat _____ on a council.
4. Once ruled Athens
5. A slave
8. Popular leader of Athens
9. Felonies
10. Magistrates
11. Decision-making body
12. _____ kings ruled Sparta
13. Region of Athens
14. Foreigners in Athens
17. Tribes were _____ into "demes"
18. Not serious
20. Past tense of "is"

LIFE IN ANCIENT GREECE

Teacher's Notes

Thousands of craftsmen throughout Greece worked with metal, jewelry, leather, ivory and clay pots made on pottery wheels often turned by slaves. The best pottery came from Athens and the decoration on vases and plates were sometimes painted by women who had the necessary skills. Many craftsmen had workshops near the "agora," the ancient marketplace in Athens.

Decorated and fired clay water pipes which fed a public fountain were exposed during excavations in the agora.

Marriage ceremonies took place at home and the bride wore a white dress and a veil like many brides today, and she was expected to give a dowry of money and goods. Rich brides rode to their new husband's home in a chariot, but most couples could only afford a cart drawn by oxen or mules. The Greeks did not have family names and sons were generally named after their father or grandfather and girls after their grandmother. Some babies were given the names of Greek heroes or gods. Babies were named when they were 10 days old and friends and relations attended the ceremony with small gifts for the baby.

Spartan weddings were less of a celebration as the bride didn't wear an attractive dress or have a procession to her new home. Throughout Greece, baby boys were preferred to girls and in Sparta, babies were often abandoned if they had defects which would prevent service in the army later in life.

Funerals were important in Ancient Greece. The bodies were prepared for burial with sweet-smelling oils before being taken to a cemetery, usually one outside the city boundaries. A coin was sometimes placed on a dead person's body to pay Charon, the ferryman who took their souls across the River Styx to Hades.

LIFE IN ANCIENT GREECE

In many ways, the main Greek cities like Athens, Sparta and Corinth were alike, for their language, religion and customs were similar. Spartans didn't like the artists and free thinkers in other parts of Greece. They led a harder existence as their way of life was organized to produce warriors for their feared armies.

At the center of the cities was the "agora," the main meeting place and market for the citizens. Many poorer families went there to obtain water from the public fountains, while richer citizens discussed current events or bought slaves from slave traders. Men did the shopping and craft shops and stalls sold all types of goods, including clothing, sandals, pottery, fish on marble slabs to keep them cold, sausage (a mixture of dog and donkey meat), fruit, flowers and produce brought in by farmers on donkey carts. Most people earned their living from agriculture. Government officials checked that shop owners did not have faulty scales or overcharge customers.

"It is a crime to refuse to take a wife."
Plato – Greek philosopher

Greek men spent little time at home during the day, but women rarely went out, spending many hours looking after their children, weaving, or doing household tasks with help from slaves. Many men in rural districts worked on farms harvesting barley or olives, while in the towns, thousands of craftsmen worked in craft shops or rooms in their own homes.

By the age of 15, many girls were married, often to men in their twenties or thirties. Marriages usually took place in January, the month dedicated to Hera, the goddess of marriage, and were arranged by the couple's fathers.

Daily life and religion were closely linked. The Greeks worshipped many gods and goddesses at shrines in their homes or in temples, which were first built by the early Greeks. If they wanted advice they went to an oracle, a shrine with a priest or priestess who had special powers to speak to the gods. The Greeks offered cakes, wine and even sacrificed animals to please a god, so prayers would be answered.

They believed the souls of the dead went to the underworld, Hades, which was ruled by Pluto. Possessions were placed in the grave to be used in the next life.

Activity Box

1. Color in the scene in the agora.

2. List the things being sold.

   _____

   _____

3. What other activity can you see?

   _____

4. In which city was life hard?

   _____

5. Describe what topics might have been discussed by men in the agora.

   _____

   _____

   _____

6. What do you think about marriages which were arranged by fathers?

   _____

   _____

7. Poor people went to the agora to buy food and get

   _____.

8. Which god ruled the underworld? _____

HOMES (1)

Teacher's Notes

The rooms in poorer homes were so small that doors onto the street often opened outwards. This meant a homeowner leaving the house would knock on his door to warn pedestrians that the door was about to be opened. The doors and shutters were made of wood and had bronze (a mixture of copper and tin) hinges before the Greeks began using iron.

Because thieves could break through mud-brick walls, they were called "wall diggers." The mud bricks were made with mud, chopped straw and animal dung, so poorer homes could have had a distinctive odor!

Homes of the rich were often decorated inside with paintings, statues and wall mosaics, or hung with woven tapestries made by the lady of the house.

Many homes were rented from wealthy owners and if a tenant couldn't pay his rent, the owner would remove the front door or cut off access to the house's well. The tenant could then take shelter with other homeless citizens in the warmth of the public baths.

The streets, sometimes paved with blocks of stone or covered with gravel, had side ditches which acted as drains, but there was no sewerage system like there was in Rome. Dark streets at night were to be avoided as thugs attacked pedestrians, who sometimes carried burning torches for light and as weapons!

HOMES (1)

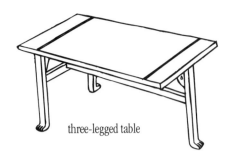

three-legged table

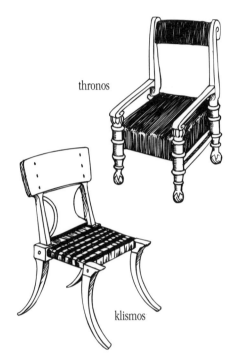

thronos

klismos

Ordinary Greeks lived in small homes on narrow, winding streets. They had two or three small rooms with beaten earth floors. The roofs had tiles of terra-cotta, a mixture of sand and baked clay, but early Greek homes probably had thatched roofs. They built their temples out of stone and marble but most house walls were usually sun-dried mud bricks or stones stuck together with mortar and reinforced with wood.

Wealthier homes were usually built of stone and brick with stone floors and separate living and dining areas for men and women. They often had a second story where bedrooms and rooms for servants and slaves were situated. They were built around a central courtyard which could contain a well for water. Richer families had a bathroom with a terra-cotta bath which had a drain leading into the street. Men ate and entertained friends in a room called the "andron" while women did the same in the "gynaikon."

Greek homes were lit with oil-burning lamps made of silver, bronze, or, in poorer homes, pottery. Heating was provided by burning charcoal in portable metal braziers. As summers were hot, windows were small with wooden shutters that could be closed to keep out the heat or the cold in winter. The windows had no glass as glass windows were invented later by the Romans.

The windows faced onto the courtyard rather than the streets where decaying rubbish, thrown there by householders, would smell until removed by gangs of slaves. Poor homes had no kitchen, so much food was cooked outside. In winter, when fires were lit inside for warmth and cooking, holes would be made at the top of the walls or tiles removed to let out the smoke.

Most furniture was made of wood and in wealthy homes tables and chairs were often inlaid with ivory, gold, or silver. Most people sat on small stools but there were two main types of chair, a high-backed chair with arms (a "thronos") for the man of the house and a smaller lady's chair with curved legs (a "klismos"). Wooden couches for reclining on while eating looked very much like beds. Tables were round, oval, or rectangular.

Activity Box

1. What was a disadvantage of inside heating in the winter?

   _____

2. What was a lady's chair called?

   _____

3. Which English word do you think comes from the Greek word "thronos"? _____

4. Where did Greek women entertain friends?

   _____

5. Why did windows face the courtyard?

   _____

HOMES (2)

Teacher's Notes

See page 20 for Homes background information and teacher's notes.

HOMES (2)

6. How did the Greeks eat their meals?

    _____

7. Why didn't the homes have glass windows?

    _____

8. Why did the citizens throw rubbish onto the street?

    _____

9. What were the temples made of?

    _____

10. Who cleaned up the streets?

    _____

List the similarities and differences between modern homes and homes in Ancient Greece.

Similarities in ancient Greek homes	Differences in ancient Greek homes
doors and shutters had hinges	street doors opened outwards

FOOD (1)

The ancient Greeks wrote many books on the art and joys of cooking, and the writer Achestratus, who lived around 400 B.C., was described as a person who "traveled the lands and seas in his desire to test the delights of the stomach."

Teacher's Notes   The famous Greek writer Homer called the people in his country "flour eaters," because they ate so much bread made from the huge quantities of imported grain.

During the hot summers, the deep roots of grapevines and olive trees could reach the water stored in the subsoils after winter rains.

Fish and other seafoods were usually eaten with sour grapes, similar to our use of lemon with fish dishes today. Lemons were unknown to the ancient Greeks.

Ancient Greek writers have written about the enormous quantities of grain available from the "black earth" plains north of the Black Sea.

FOOD (1)

Because much of central Greece is mountainous with poor soil, farms developed near the coast on the few areas of fertile land. As sufficient crops could not be grown to provide food for the whole population, supplies had to be imported from other places around the Mediterranean Sea.

These imports would often be in exchange for olives and wine. Like walnut and almond trees, grapevines and olive trees grew wild but could also be cultivated on the lower slopes of the mountains on soil not fertile enough for grain crops. Olive oil and wine were transported around Greece or exported in large pottery jars called amphorae. Olive oil was used in cooking many foods.

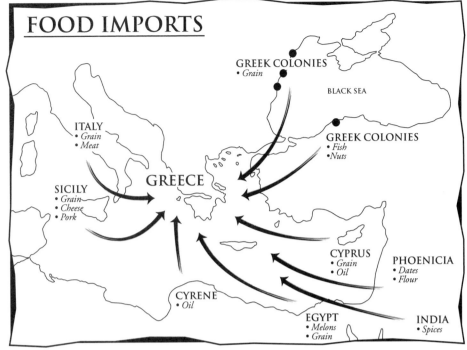

FOOD IMPORTS

- GREEK COLONIES
  - Grain
- BLACK SEA
- ITALY
  - Grain
  - Meat
- GREEK COLONIES
  - Fish
  - Nuts
- SICILY
  - Grain
  - Cheese
  - Pork
- GREECE
- CYPRUS
  - Grain
  - Oil
- PHOENICIA
  - Dates
  - Flour
- CYRENE
  - Oil
- EGYPT
  - Melons
  - Grain
- INDIA
  - Spices

Though rich families sometimes ate meat from wild pigs, sheep and cattle, there were only a few areas of Greece which had enough rainfall and soil fertile enough to grow grass for grazing cattle. The rich usually ate fresh fish and other seafoods for they were plentiful in the seas around Greece. Fish were also salted and dried in the sun or preserved in oil and vinegar for the winter. Because of the abundant supply, seafood was also eaten by poorer families who lived in many Greek settlements on the coast.

Use the information above and the following words to complete the passage.

life	**grow**	**fleets**	**India**	**fresh**	**Sicily**	**salted**	**infertile**	**imported**	**quantities**
feed	**soil**	**grain**	**olive**	**lower**	**storms**	**Cyprus**	**several**	**valuable**	**mountains**

Crops weren't grown high in the _____[1] as the soil was _____[2], but farmers

could cultivate _____[3] trees on the _____[4] slopes where _____[5]

was too poor for _____[6] crops. Because farmers couldn't _____[7] sufficient food

to _____[8] the population, large _____[9] of food were _____[10].

Spices came from _____[11] and cheese from _____[12]

while grain came from _____[13] parts of the Mediterranean. From

Cyrene and _____[14] came oil, a product so _____[15]

in ancient Greek daily _____[16]. Many Greeks ate _____[17]

fish but also _____[18] them to preserve for winter when frequent

_____[19] prevented fishing _____[20] from leaving port.

Examples of amphorae—used to store wine and oil.

FOOD (2)

Teacher's Notes

In the fish plate coloring activity, the students could color using their own choice of colors purely as an art exercise, or they could use the colors most common at that time on pottery paintings from Corinth and Athens—reddish brown shapes on the black background or the reverse. The reddish brown was the color of the baked clay and clay slip paint mixed with wood ash gave the black color.

FOOD (2)

Color in the plate.

Ancient Greek fish plate probably used for serving fish. The bowl in the center held a spicy sauce.

Ancient Greece

FOOD (3)

Teacher's Notes

The ancient Greeks didn't have napkins. They wiped their hands on bread which they then fed to the dogs. Spoons were used for liquid dishes like stews or soups and knives were used to cut up fish or meat, but forks were unknown. The Greeks ate their food as they reclined on couches, as did the Romans in later years.

The Greeks began to cultivate mushrooms in the fifth century B.C. and thought they grew because of the thunder in showers. About this time, melons were imported from Egypt, but they were very expensive.

Most people kept hens for fresh eggs. Rich families enjoyed eggs from hens but also ate eggs from geese and game birds. Owls, believed to be the birds of Athena, the goddess of wisdom, were never killed by hunters. The Greeks also thought olives were a gift from Athena who, in legend, struck the Acropolis rock with her spear and the first olive tree grew on that spot.

The famous black broth from Sparta, believed to have been made from pork stock, salt and vinegar, was well known throughout Ancient Greece, but not popular with many visitors to Sparta.

Bees were kept in terra-cotta hives and honey was used to make mead, an alcoholic drink made from water and fermented honey.

FOOD (3)

Poor Greek families generally ate barley porridge, soups, or dishes made from vegetables like peas and beans. Lettuces and cabbages were expensive and rarely eaten. Cakes and bread were made from grain and baked in dome-shaped ovens. Both rich and poor drank wine, though poor citizens could not afford as much. Bread was often dipped into watered-down wine and eaten with fruit such as dates or figs. Barley was the most important grain crop. Wheat was only grown in the few areas where the soil was good which made it expensive. Fresh fruit or fruit dried in the sun was popular. While wine was favored among the rich, most people drank water or milk from goats, the most common domestic animal. Bees were kept for honey which was used to sweeten food as the Greeks had no knowledge of sugar cane or sugar beet. They did not know about rice, potatoes, or tomatoes either.

Because Greece has a mild climate with favorable weather for most of the year, food was often cooked outdoors on an open fire or in pottery ovens which could be carried outside. Birds and wild animals such as quail, pheasants, foxes, wild pigs, deer, bears and hares were hunted for food using dogs.

Additional Activity

Color the foods eaten by the ancient Greeks, then write the names in alphabetical order in the second set of boxes.

Porridge	Olives	Pork	Peas
Honey	Eggs	Cheese	Dates
Bread	Mushrooms	Fish	Chicken

1.	2.	3.	4.
5.	6.	7.	8.
9.	10.	11.	12.

FOOD (4)

Teacher's Notes

See pages 24, 26 and 28 for Food background information and teacher's notes.

FOOD (4)

Across

1. The Greeks didn't know about this basic food.
3. _____ families ate little meat.
5. These could not grow in infertile soil.
6. Common vegetable eaten by everyone.
7. Expensive vegetables.
10. Food in plentiful supply.
11. Made into bread and cakes.
12. Would prevent fishing in winter.
14. Used to preserve fish.
16. Used to preserve fish.
17. The Greeks didn't have _____ tomatoes.
18. Used to sweeten food.
19. The _____ families ate deer meat (venison).

Down

2. Baked in ovens and sweetened with honey
3. Birds hunted for food.
4. Common domestic animal
5. Dairy food
8. Exported oil to Greece
9. Exported grain to Greece
10. Most _____ farmland was near the coast.
13. The Greeks did not know about this.
15. This had to be fertile to grow grass for cattle.

FARMING (1)

Teacher's Notes

Agriculture was the most important aspect of the economies of almost every country in the world until the Industrial Revolution in the 19th century exerted its influence.

Most farming plots were very small and one sixth century B.C. survey of the wealth of citizens of Athens showed that even rich men only had mixed plots of grain and vines from about 20–30 hectares in size (1 hectare = 10,000 m^2). In Sparta, the largest and most fertile areas were shared among the citizens and run for them by slaves.

Greek society did not have laws ensuring a father's eldest son inherited all his property (primogeniture), so when a landowner died his property was shared among all his sons. Over the years, this meant that farm plots became smaller and smaller until some became too small to support a family.

The Greeks saw nothing to admire in having to work for a living, but farming was viewed as a most respectable way of life if one had to work.

When food was short in Athens in 591 B.C., the city-state's leader, Solon, passed a law which said that farmers could only sell their crops in Athens. The laws didn't include olives, for Greek farmers, even today, have always produced more than the country needed.

Ancient Greece

FARMING (1)

As in most of the early civilizations, agriculture in Ancient Greece was the most important occupation and employed most people. Around 6000 B.C., people from the eastern Mediterranean regions settled in eastern Greece and began to farm the land. In the following centuries, it became traditional for Greek freemen to own land and their wealth was indicated by the size of their property and the number of animals they owned. Some smaller farmers could not afford slaves and just managed to scrape a living for their families. If there was a crop failure, poor farmers could not usually support themselves and would have to work for their landowners on larger estates or seek work in the city. There were no huge farming estates run by hundreds of slaves as in the later Roman Empire, but there were slaves used on the larger farms owned by noble families or rich landowners from the cities.

Coin from a Greek colony in southern Italy. A grain motif shows the importance of this crop.

Copy of vase in the British Museum showing the olive harvest. Olives were picked by hand or dislodged from the trees with sticks. This pot was made in Athens about 520 B.C.

With so many mountains, soil in Greece was generally poor. Most of the good farmland was near the coast, though there were well-watered areas like one about 20 km northwest of Corinth which was famous for its fruit and vegetables. Bread was the most important food, so barley, wheat (in more fertile areas) and other grains were the main crops. Athens could only grow about 30 percent of its grain requirements, so large quantities had to be imported. Olives were also an important crop. Poor farmers could plant olive trees for they would grow on poor soil. Some olives were eaten but most were pressed to obtain oil for cooking and lighting, or for export to sell or barter for other goods. In the city-state of Athens it was a criminal offence to dig up an olive tree, possibly because they took so long to mature, but probably because of their importance to the economy.

Activity Box

1. The most important crops were grains and
   _____.

2. When did early settlers first cultivate the land in Greece?
   _____

3. Which city-state grew fine fruit and vegetables?
   _____

4. Why was olive oil so important?
   _____
   _____

5. Olive trees grow quickly. True or False?
   _____

6. How did the Greeks pick their olives?
   _____
   _____

7. What was the most important food made from farm produce?
   _____

8. Which Greeks could own land?
   _____

9. Why could olive trees grow on mountain slopes?
   _____

10. Which city-state had to import grain?
    _____

FARMING (2)

Many fields around Greece were plowed several times a year to loosen up the top layers of hard soil and rocks. Plato, the great Greek philosopher, referred to the land as a "fleshless skeleton" where the surface rocks resembled bones.

Teacher's Notes Early in their history, before they conquered the Messenians around 750 B.C., the Spartans had defeated the Laconians. Laconia had large areas of very fertile land and both the Messenians and the Laconians, because they were conquered people, were not free citizens. They had to work on the land, virtually as slaves called "helots."

Many horses were grazed in Thessaly in northern Greece where rich pastures were plentiful.

Women on the farms dyed the sheep's wool and spun it into yarn which was then woven into cloth to make clothing.

During the years of the tyrants in Greece (ca. 650–500 B.C.), one Athenian ruler, Pisistratus, helped smaller farmers by creating a state loan fund, and injected more money into the scheme in later years by placing a tax of about 5 percent on agricultural produce, the first known direct taxation of citizens.

The grapes were usually trodden underfoot in large tubs called vats. The last drops of grape juice were then forced out in a wine press and allowed to ferment into wine. A press was also used to obtain oil from olives.

Treading the grapes

Olive press

Stones to increase downward pressure

FARMING (2)

1 Because summers were very hot and dry with little rain, grain crops were sown in the autumn, around October, so they would grow during mild, wet winter months. One worker steered a simple wooden plow drawn by oxen while another man walked behind sowing the seeds by hand.

2 The crops were harvested in April or May before the fierce heat of the summer could damage the ears of grain. The farm workers used curved tools called sickles to cut down the grain stalks. The sickle blades were made of bronze but in later years, around 700 B.C., the forging of iron improved rapidly and iron blades were used. After harvesting, fields were sometimes left fallow (no crop planted) to give the soil a chance to recover.

3 The cut grain was separated from the stalks (threshed) by driving mules or oxen over it on a stone-paved floor. The wind carried away the chaff, which is the light outer cover of the grain.

4 The grain could also be separated from the chaff on windy days in a process called winnowing. The grain would be tossed into the air and the chaff was gradually blown away. The grain husks would then be removed by pounding the grain with a tool called a pestle in a bowl called a mortar.

Olives and grapes were harvested in late summer, around August or September. Both were grown on lower mountain slopes to leave more fertile land on the plains for grain and vegetable crops. Good grazing land for horses and cattle was scarce so cows were kept for milk rather than meat. Goats and sheep grazed on poorer pastures and sheep were mainly raised for wool and milk, as well as for meat. Goats were kept for milk and young goats and pigs for meat. Oxen were generally used as draft animals and mules or donkeys for transportation. Chickens were kept for eggs and bees for honey. The hides of some farm animals were used for leather.

Activity Box

1. Color the pictures of the grain harvest stages.

2. Discuss with a partner any similarities or differences you can find when comparing modern farming with farming in Ancient Greece. Then collate information to make a class list under two headings on the board.

TRADE (1)

Teacher's Notes

Coins first appeared in the kingdom of Lydia in Asia Minor. It wasn't a Greek settlement but the Greeks soon copied the idea of making coins and in later years even the smaller city-states were issuing their own coins. The first coins were made of electrum, a natural light-yellow alloy of gold and silver. The earlier Greeks used silver for most of their coins and a round flat shape soon became the accepted form. Athens controlled one of the few precious metal deposits on the mainland—the silver mines in Laurium. Sparta used iron rods and didn't use coins for three centuries after the other Greek states.

Another reason why there was less trade along land routes in mainland Greece was the fact that most Greeks lived less than 70 km from the sea, so they were a seafaring people.

Pirates would sometimes cast captured crew members into the sea or sell them as slaves in far-off lands so that the unfortunate sailors might never see their families again. In the fifth century B.C., the powerful Athenian navy cleared most of the pirates from the seas around the Greek coastline, and merchant fleets were protected by warships called triremes, because Athens depended so much on its grain supplies from the Black Sea colonies. This grain was paid for with silver from the silver mines at Laurium in Attica, the region around Athens.

Several Greek colonies sent metals to Greece, as they were in great demand by various city-states who were often at war with each other and needed metal to forge weapons and armor. Greece imported many goods from the Persian Empire even though they were often on unfriendly terms.

Our word "copper" is derived from the Greek word Kyprios (Cyprus). The island of Cyprus was noted for its copper mines which provided the valuable metal to the Greek mainland city-states.

Timber for shipbuilding had to be imported, for very few trees grew in the southern areas of the Greek mainland or on the Greek islands in the Aegean Sea.

Ancient Greece

TRADE (1)

Archaeologists have discovered Greek coins, vases and sculptures in countries around the Mediterranean Sea—evidence of trade with other nations. Though the Greeks began to buy goods with money around 600 B.C., they also exchanged one kind of goods for another in a system called barter. The Greeks usually exported olives, wine, painted pottery, statues, metalwork and books. Wine and olives were produced in abundance but other products of the soil were, at times, banned from being sold to potential enemies.

The Greek city-states also traded with each other and with Greek colonies established around the Mediterranean, such as Syracuse and Marseilles (Massilia). Trade by land with Greece wasn't common because rough mountain roads made passage difficult for mule carts and there was a threat from robber bands in the hills. Thus, many Greek cities on the coast traded by sea, but merchants had to be wary of pirates lurking in coves along the coasts.

Because of the poor soil and barren mountains in large areas of mainland Greece, food and other supplies had to be imported. Linen for sails and copper and tin to make bronze for weapons and armor in the early Mycenaean age were two essential imports. Unfortunately, slaves from outside the Greek world were another common cargo.

Activity Box

1. Use the notes and your own words to complete the passage.

   The Greeks traded with their own _____[1] around the _____[2] of the

   Mediterranean Sea. Trade on land was very _____[3] because of the poor _____[4]

   and the problem of attacks by _____[5] gangs. Merchant ships were often _____[6] by

   pirates who would steal the _____[7] carried by the ships. The _____[8] into Greece

   included cloth for _____[9] and metals to make _____[10] for weapons. Ships also

   brought in _____[11] who were not _____[12] and had to _____[13] long

   hours as servants in Greek _____[14] or on the _____[15] in farming areas.

2. Illustrate some of these important imports into Ancient Greece.

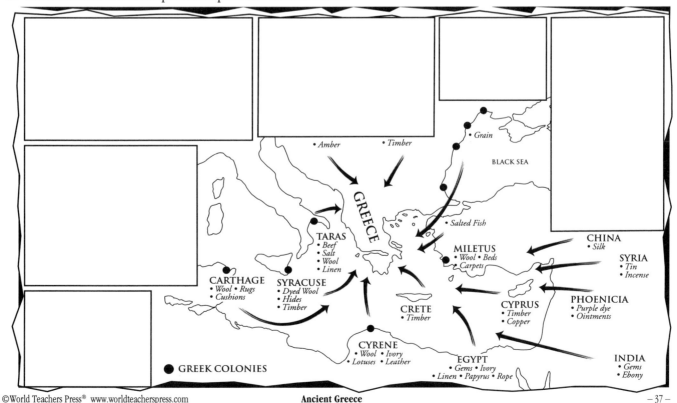

TRADE (2)

Teacher's Notes

Though merchants were individuals seeking profit for themselves, the Greek historian, Plutarch, remarked that "the calling of a merchant was held in honor in early Greece."

Greek merchants traded with the Phoenicians, who were the first traders to sell cheap goods to a large market, the basis of modern trade.

A wrecked Bronze Age merchant ship discovered in the eastern Mediterranean was loaded with copper and probably heading for a Mycenaean port.

A Greek poet called Hermippos listed some of the goods imported into Peiraieus, the port of ancient Athens. Many of them are shown on the map in Trade (1).

The Mediterranean offered several advantages to the merchant ships sailing its waters: it had hardly any tides, the indented coasts provided shelter and harbors for the ships, the sea was usually very calm in the summer months, and there were great island chains between Greece and Asia Minor so that ships did not have to cross large expanses of open sea.

The earliest Greek poem, Homer's "Iliad," tells of the grief of sailors carried out to sea in sudden storms, even though merchant ships in these early times generally hugged the coast to avoid such perils.

Thales, a Greek from the Greek colony of Miletus, studied Egyptian methods of astronomy and surveying and devised a method whereby the captain of a ship could navigate by the stars and also find out how far he was from land.

Experts believe that some examples of a "kerkouroi," a ship with both sails and oars, are shown on vase paintings from those times.

TRADE (2)

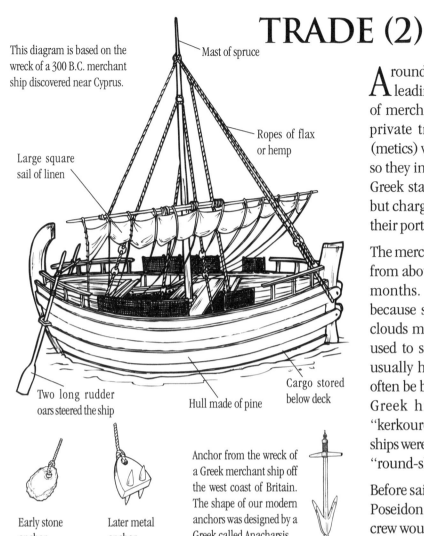

This diagram is based on the wreck of a 300 B.C. merchant ship discovered near Cyprus.

Mast of spruce

Ropes of flax or hemp

Large square sail of linen

Two long rudder oars steered the ship

Hull made of pine

Cargo stored below deck

Early stone anchor

Later metal anchor

Anchor from the wreck of a Greek merchant ship off the west coast of Britain. The shape of our modern anchors was designed by a Greek called Anacharsis.

Around 500 B.C., Athens and Corinth were the two leading trading centers. Athens had a large fleet of merchant ships which were owned by individual private traders. Many merchants were foreigners (metics) who were not permitted to own land in Greece so they invested their money in goods and ships. The Greek states didn't interfere with the private traders but charged customs duties for use of the facilities in their ports.

The merchants sailed around the Mediterranean ports from about April to September, the northern summer months. Winter months were avoided if possible because storms could blow up suddenly and storm clouds meant they couldn't see the stars which they used to steer their course at night. Merchant ships usually had no oarsmen, only a sail, so they would often be becalmed when the wind dropped, but some Greek historians wrote about a ship called a "kerkouroi" which had a sail and oars. Many trading ships were small until the sixth century B.C. when large "round-ships" were built to carry bulk cargoes.

Before sailing, a merchant would pray or offer gifts to Poseidon, the Greek god of the sea, so his ship and its crew would be protected from storms or pirates.

Activity Box

Read both pages on trade in Ancient Greece and answer the questions.

1. What were foreigners in Greece called?

   _____

2. Precious stones were imported from

   _____ and _____.

3. Greeks began to trade with coins around

   _____ B.C.

4. A merchant ship with sail and oars was a

   _____.

5. The modern name for the Greek colony

   Massilia is _____.

6. Rough roads and _____

   reduced trade within Greece.

7. What happened to the design of merchant ships in the sixth century B.C.?

   _____

   _____

8. Trading ships sailed mainly in the

   _____ months.

9. Which Mediterranean island was an important source of copper for Greece?

   _____

10. Exchanging goods for other goods is a type of trade called

   _____

EDUCATION

Teacher's Notes

The wealthy boy's slave, a "paidagogos," taught him good manners, could punish him if he was naughty, and even test him on his school work.

Girls were usually taught household duties at home by their mothers, though some from wealthy homes were also taught to read and write by private tutors. An educated mother may have read simple stories like Aesop's fables to her children.

In some European countries, such as Germany, secondary schools are still called "gymnasiums."

At seven, Spartan boys boarded at military schools where they were often whipped to prepare them for the pain and fear of battle. Aggression was part of Greek life, for honor and glory for many citizens came from conquering other Greek city-states.

The importance of physical education in Ancient Greece was indicated in their description of someone who wasn't very clever as a person who "doesn't even know how to read or swim."

School classes took place during daylight hours, for a law forbade children from going to or coming home from school in the dark. A Greek education was even valued outside Greece, and in the later Roman Empire many Roman boys were educated in schools in Athens until they closed down around 600 A.D. Though education had to be paid for, the cost was small as teachers were generally disliked.

In the classical period (480–323 B.C.), older Athenian pupils learned the four math operations—addition, multiplication, subtraction and division—and were also taught how to use fractions in order to train them for public life. A knowledge of Greek history and famous writers in Greek literature like Homer and Euripides helped a person to be seen as an educated man.

Education was valued in Ancient Greece and the great philosopher, Plato, spoke in favor of "children's parks filled with educational games," a policy supported by educators and social planners today.

EDUCATION

Education in Ancient Greece was primarily for boys, who began school at six or seven years of age. Boys from wealthier families would be accompanied by a personal slave who carried their writing tablets, made sure they paid attention in class and prevented them from being truant. Education wasn't free and the private teacher, who would be paid for his tuition, held his classes in the mornings, for afternoons were devoted to physical activities. From the ages of 7–14, students went to primary school and from 14–18 to the gymnasium (secondary school). At 12, physical education became the most important instruction in schools. The boys exercised in the nude and the timetable included discus throwing, javelin, running, jumping and wrestling.

The schools in the city-states varied. Education in Sparta was very strict and the State would take boys away from their families at the age of seven or eight. Until the age of 14, Spartan students learned only the basics of reading and writing which were considered less important than military training. Physical training also applied to Spartan girls, a practice frowned on by other Greek states. Sparta wanted physically strong young men for its powerful army and strong young women to bear healthy babies.

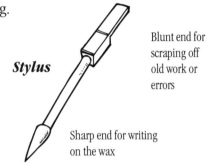

Stylus

Blunt end for scraping off old work or errors

Sharp end for writing on the wax

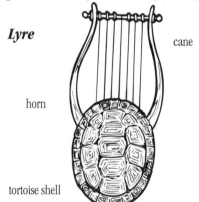

Lyre

cane

horn

tortoise shell

Most poor children had no education and probably never learned to read or write. In the early school years, students were taught reading and writing by a "grammatist" and wrote their work on wax tablets using a stylus, a tool made of wood, bone, or metal. In the later years, students were taught math, perhaps geometry, by using a bead frame called an abacus, small stones, or even their fingers. They learned the poems of famous Greek writers like Homer by heart as teachers read them out from scrolls of paper made from the papyrus plant. Boys from wealthy families had private music tutors who taught them how to play the lyre, flute, or pipes.

Schoolchildren probably had no desks, as vase paintings show them sitting on wooden stools holding their tablets. Classes were small, around 10 students, and teachers imposed discipline by the use of corporal punishment. Emphasis was placed on rote learning.

Activity Box

1. What aspects of ancient Greek education do you like or dislike?

   _____

2. Work with a partner/group to make a wax tablet using the following procedure.

   (a)   Find a shallow lid from a small box.

   (b)   Use soft modeling clay (warmed in the sun) or melted candle wax to fill up the lid.

   (c)   Use a sharp wood stick to carve out a message to a partner.

   (d)   Use the blunt end of your writing tool to follow the advice of Ovid, an ancient Roman writer, who said, "Whenever you write, make sure all previous letters have been erased from your tablet."

   wax

   lid

HEALTH

Teacher's Notes

Hippocrates taught that "every disease has its own nature, and arises from external causes," and that diseases were not a punishment handed down by the gods. He realized open wounds could become infected, but didn't know why. He also believed the body had natural defenses to fight disease, something we now know to be true. His writings introduced the concept of preventing sickness through diet and life-style, and he suggested that the weather and drinking water could affect the health of the citizens. "Nature of Man" by Hippocrates describes how illnesses were caused by an imbalance of liquids in the body, a reason why later Greek doctors sometimes drew blood from patients' arms for they believed blood contained disease.

Public health physicians working for the State had to announce their qualifications at the "ekklesia," the people's assembly.

One herb, hyssop, used for coughs and chest infections, was still in use in the 20th century.

In the third century B.C., the physician Herophilus was interested in the medicinal qualities of new drugs and also developed a diagnostic method using different pulse beats. Even after Ancient Greece was conquered by the Romans, the Greeks were regarded as the most important teachers of medical knowledge.

Sick people often made terra-cotta or bronze models to show physicians or priests which part of the body was affected. Models of ears, noses, breasts, legs and eyes have been unearthed in archaeological excavations, especially those which uncovered ancient shrines.

Additional Activity

Many doctors around the world swear a modern version of the Hippocratic Oath before they practice their profession. Find the modern version and discuss any differences.

HEALTH

Though the ancient Greeks had a god of medicine, Asclepius, they were the first people to separate medical treatment from methods which used religion, myth and witchcraft. This happened around 400 B.C. when the teachings of Hippocrates were generally accepted by physicians. Hippocrates was the son of a physician and was born and practiced on the island of Kos, though he also appears to have traveled widely spreading his beliefs.

Hippocratic bench

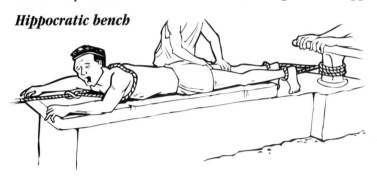

Broken bones were pulled into place and then splints used to help them to set.

We refer to Hippocrates as the "father of medicine." He studied his patient's symptoms before making a diagnosis and made notes on the effects of different medicines, thus treating medicine more scientifically. His Hippocratic Oath, associated with his teachings but probably not written by him, described the moral standards for doctors and has helped physicians, then and now, to enjoy a respected place in society.

There were many private doctors in Greece, but Athens also had a public health service with doctors chosen and paid by the State. Doctors performed operations with simple instruments made from bronze, but since there were no anesthetics, they were painful and patients often died from infection or shock. Dentists used fillings of gold or even lead; they weren't aware of lead's poisonous properties. Sick people often made sacrifices at a temple and then slept there overnight, hoping to be cured by the next morning. Temple priests were Greece's earliest doctors and they treated diseases with a mixture of herbs, diets, magic, exercise, or rest.

Excavated metal surgical instruments.

Many poor children suffered from diseases like rickets through lack of vitamins, and the doubtful qualities of drinking water led to many stomach complaints. Ancient Greek doctors, of course, had no solution for disease epidemics, and a plague caused by flea-ridden rats in Athens around 430 B.C. killed thousands, including the great statesman Pericles.

Activity Box

Use the given words to complete part of one translation of the Hippocratic code of conduct.

go	act	give	asked	secret	benefit	females	divulge	corruption	professional
all	men	hear	slaves	houses	counsel	abstain	medicine	connection	

"I will _____[1] no deadly _____[2] to anyone if _____[3], nor

suggest any such _____[4]; . . . Into whatever _____[5] I enter, I will

_____[6] into them for the _____[7] of the sick, and will _____[8] from

every voluntary _____[9] of mischief and _____[10]; and further from the seduction of

_____[11] or males, of freemen and _____[12]. . . . Whatever, in connection with my

_____[13] practice or not in _____[14] with it, I see or _____[15], in the

life of _____[16], which ought not to be spoken of abroad, I will not _____[17], as

reckoning that _____[18] such should be kept _____[19]."

A WOMAN'S LIFE

Teacher's Notes

It is strange that despite their worship of goddesses as guardians of justice, wisdom and peace, the attitude of the Greeks to their own women was so different.

Greek women had restricted citizenship rights for the purpose of marriage and motherhood and some religious festivals. They weren't full citizens but could pass on citizenship to their sons.

In Sparta, women were highly honored, though they did not have any political rights and could not work in government positions.

The playwrights Aristophanes and Euripides both thought that the status of women in society needed to be improved. After the Peloponnesian War (27 years of conflict), social attitudes changed and all levels of society, including women, enjoyed more rights and freedom than before.

Greek women used ground chalk or even white lead as face powder, since they didn't know that lead was poisonous. The earliest records on the use of perfume date back over 5,000 years to the ancient Egyptians. The Greeks believed that the perfume from roses worn around the head relieved headaches.

The young boy slaves or girls at symposiums (male drinking parties) were chosen for their beauty. Foreign or low-born women called "hetairai" entertained the guests at these male parties, for they were often educated foreigners trained in dancing and playing music.

Before spinning, a sheep's fleece was steeped in hot water to clean and remove some of the grease in the wool. The Greeks made dyes to color cloth by soaking plants in hot water or used dyes made from seashells or insects. They used the red roots of the madder vine for red, oak bark for brown, and for blue they used the leaves of woad, a plant of the mustard family. A chemical called alum was used to prevent the color coming out when a cloth was washed. Wool was always dyed whereas linen was left white.

Additional Activity

Greek women made their perfumes by soaking leaves or petals from plants like roses, cinnamon, lilies, lavender and marjoram in warm oil. Make your own perfumed oils by:

(a) Soaking your choice in warm oil in a jar.

(b) Leave the jar in the sun (stir occasionally).

(c) Strain off the plants.

A WOMAN'S LIFE

warp

threads weighted
with stones

Loom

In most Greek homes was a room called the "gynaikon" where women gathered to work on their looms, entertain friends, or supervise their children. Women never attended the symposiums (male drinking parties), even those held in their own homes. Well-born Athenian women didn't have a social life with their husbands, for female slaves or others provided service and entertainment at the popular symposiums.

Greek women made the family clothes, curtains, couch covers and cushions for the wooden furniture from woven wool or flax. More expensive cloths like silk were bought at the marketplace. Like men, women wore a loose tunic called a "chiton" with a cloak over the top. Women wore a full-length chiton whereas a man's was usually only knee-length. The woman's chiton was often dyed red or yellow, tied at the waist and fastened with shoulder brooches or long bronze shoulder pins. Broad-brimmed hats were worn to protect their faces from the hot sun. Many perfume and cosmetic jars have been excavated as Greek women used skin creams and believed in using different perfumes on different parts of the body.

with pony tail

bun with
ribbons

with head scarf

Women could not take any part in politics for they weren't recognized as citizens, so they couldn't vote. Very few had an education or an occupation outside the home, unless they were priestesses. They had to obey all males in the family, even their sons! A woman was usually married at 15 to a husband chosen by her father. Assisted by slaves, women worked in the kitchen grinding barley to make bread and porridge, the loaves being baked in fired clay ovens. Poorer women collected water from public fountains and thus were able to socialize, but in wealthier homes slaves did this task. Farmers' wives were also expected to help on the farm but their husbands were not expected to help with household tasks.

An Athenian woman could not own any property except her personal belongings, unless there were no male heirs when her husband died. Spartan women could inherit land in their own right—until it was found that women owned $^2/_5$ of the land and this led to a political upheaval!

Activity Box

Imagine you are going to speak at the "ekklesia," the Assembly of the people, in favor of improving women's rights. With a partner, draft the points you would raise and place them in order of importance.

1. _____
2. _____
3. _____
4. _____
5. _____
6. _____

ARTS AND CRAFTS (1)

By 1000 B.C., craftsmen in Athens were producing beautiful painted pottery and were the leaders in this art form. Many crafts, including pottery, were practiced in families, with apprentices often learning skills from a master craftsman, who was their father.

Teacher's Notes   The Sumerians of around 3200 B.C. used wheels for their chariots and also for pottery making. When Greek potters designed a faster wheel, they needed a smoother clay, so they mixed the excavated raw clay with water. When the harder particles sank to the bottom they filtered the solution, perhaps through cloth, to obtain the finer clay. This was then allowed to dry out before use. The best black-figured pottery was made in Athens, where red-figured pottery was invented.

Some pots were painted after firing in the kiln, but over the thousands of years the quality of the paint work has deteriorated.

Ancient pottery can be dated by a process called "thermoluminescence" (TL). A small piece drilled from a vase or statue is crushed and sieved to extract quartz crystals, which are then placed into a photomultiplier machine. When electrons in the crystals move back into place, light is given off. The amount of light emitted indicates the age of the pottery.

Potters made a huge range of items and a portable terra-cotta toilet seat has even been unearthed! As early as the fifth century B.C. they were producing black-glazed tableware, plates, wine goblets and jugs.

By the fourth century B.C., red- and black-figured pottery became less popular, and artists turned to painting murals on walls in public buildings and palaces, one of the greatest skills possessed by the ancient Greeks.

Pottery forms

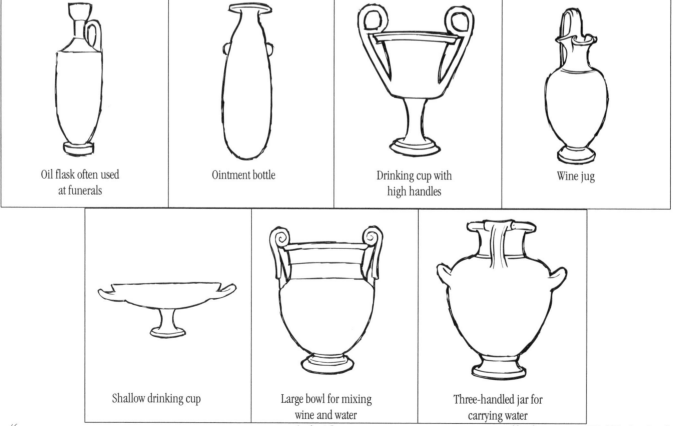

Oil flask often used at funerals

Ointment bottle

Drinking cup with high handles

Wine jug

Shallow drinking cup

Large bowl for mixing wine and water

Three-handled jar for carrying water

ARTS AND CRAFTS (1)

Pottery, designs on coins and jewelry, sculpture, painting and fine metalwork were all examples of Greek artistic skills. Apart from potters, craftsmen worked in silver, gold, bronze, glass, leather and ivory.

The best Greek pottery came from Athens with its high-quality clay, and Athenian vases with their fine designs were exported to all parts of the Greek world and to Greek settlements as far apart as France and Asia Minor. The vase paintings were usually human figures, gods and mythical heroes, animals, or geometric designs. These paintings have told us much about everyday life in Ancient Greece for fired pottery can survive for thousands of years.

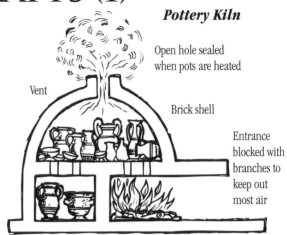

Pottery Kiln

Open hole sealed when pots are heated

Vent

Brick shell

Entrance blocked with branches to keep out most air

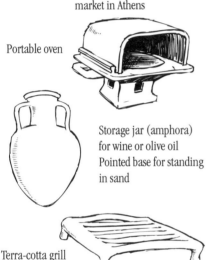

Terra-cotta household items excavated in the market in Athens

Portable oven

Storage jar (amphora) for wine or olive oil Pointed base for standing in sand

Terra-cotta grill

Potters worked in small groups on pottery wheels which were sometimes turned by slaves. When the vases were dry and firm they were brush painted with a clay solution, sometimes by female artists who were poorly paid. In the earlier black-figured pottery, the potter drew his picture on the damp vase with a sharp stick in preparation for the painting when the clay was hard. The paint was a mixture of clay, water and wood ash (for a black finish).

In the kiln, the hot gases sucked out the oxygen in the red clay and turned the pots black. When the kiln was opened the unpainted parts absorbed oxygen and turned red again. All painted figures or designs remained black. When red-figured pottery became popular in later years, the background was black and the red figures or designs were obtained with a clay solution dyed with red oxide or left unpainted. Any white decoration was a mixture of white clay and water.

Apart from elegant vases, potters made everyday items like cups, water jugs and hipbaths.

Activity Box

Color the figures and designs in vase A in black on an orange-red background. In vase B, the background is black and the figures an orange-red.

(A) Black-figured vase   (B) Red-figured vase

Fishmonger cutting up fish for a customer

ARTS AND CRAFTS (2)

Teacher's Notes

Furnaces needed to be heated only to around 1090⁰C to make bronze, but as high as 2010⁰C to make iron.

To make bronze, the Greeks imported copper from Cyprus, the main source, and Asia Minor, and tin from Spain, France and even Cornwall in Britain. Greek trading ships have been found carrying large bronze statues made from imported ores.

Despite their fearsome military reputation, the Spartans had craftsmen who excelled in making articles of bronze.

Before the Greeks could melt iron, articles made of this metal were wrought and not cast in molds. This process meant the iron was heated until red hot and then beaten into shape to make wrought iron.

As bronze was a valued metal, many of the large public statues were later melted down and re-used to make other items.

Additional Activity

Refer to various reference sources and write a paragraph on the Chalybes. You may find information under the heading "Iron—history of."

ARTS AND CRAFTS (2)

Around 3000 B.C., Greek metalworkers could melt the softer metals, silver, gold, copper and tin (to make bronze) in simple furnaces, using charcoal, but couldn't raise temperatures high enough to melt iron. Then, around 1050 B.C., they learned the method from the Chalybes, whose ironsmiths lived on the eastern shores of the Black Sea.

The Chalybes, believed to be the world's first craftsmen working in iron, lived near mountain ranges rich in this metal.

Once the technique had been mastered by the Greeks, iron proved to be less expensive and more plentiful than the ores needed to make bronze.

Molten bronze flowed more easily than copper so it was easier to pour into molds to make solid objects like small statues. Bronze was also harder when it cooled and therefore was suitable for tools or weapons. When metal workers in bronze experimented with different amounts of copper and tin in any mixture, they gradually found that less tin made the bronze tougher and not as brittle.

Clay-lined brick furnace

The molten iron would be mixed with ash and cinders which had to be removed.

Goatskin bellows to increase the heat

Layers of charcoal and iron ore placed in furnace

Tongs to take out the molten iron

Hammer to beat out any impurities in the molten metal

Furnace similar to one shown on a vase painting.

Bronze was used to make common household items like mirrors, vases and kitchen utensils, but was also used to make armor and statues. Apart from finding how to melt iron, Greek craftsmen also learned other skills from their neighbors in Asia Minor. These included bronze hollow casting where the article was not a solid cast like many of the small statues and other objects.

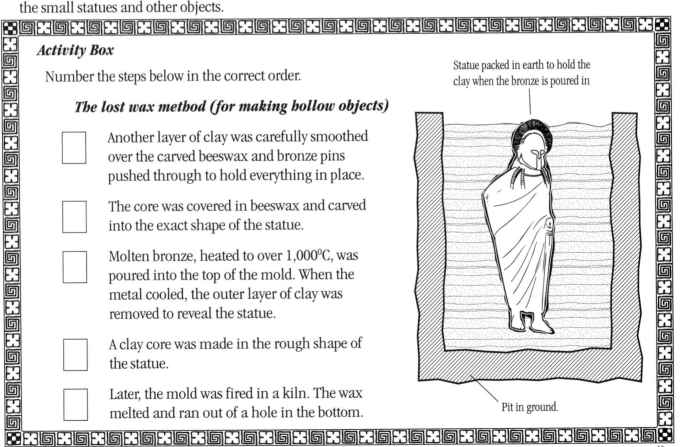

Activity Box

Number the steps below in the correct order.

The lost wax method (for making hollow objects)

☐ Another layer of clay was carefully smoothed over the carved beeswax and bronze pins pushed through to hold everything in place.

☐ The core was covered in beeswax and carved into the exact shape of the statue.

☐ Molten bronze, heated to over 1,000°C, was poured into the top of the mold. When the metal cooled, the outer layer of clay was removed to reveal the statue.

☐ A clay core was made in the rough shape of the statue.

☐ Later, the mold was fired in a kiln. The wax melted and ran out of a hole in the bottom.

Statue packed in earth to hold the clay when the bronze is poured in

Pit in ground.

ARTS AND CRAFTS (3)

Teacher's Notes

Though gold and silver were commonly used in jewelry, the two metals were rarely used together in the same article. Not many articles made from these two metals have survived for, like copper, they were often melted down and re-used. They were also stolen by tomb thieves and conquerors like the Romans, who seized thousands of items made from gold and silver.

Around 482 B.C., an exceptionally rich vein of silver was found in the mines at Laurium, and by the end of the fifth century B.C., about 20,000 slaves were working there under appalling conditions in what were once copper mines. Laurium was about 40 km southeast of Athens and silver from its mines helped to build the fine Athenian navy.

The slave workers at Laurium were often in danger from poisonous gases or possible rock falls in the underground tunnels.

ARTS AND CRAFTS (3)

Finger ring by skilled craftsman

The precious metals, gold and silver, were used for a variety of items such as jewelry, coins, decoration on statues and luxury articles purchased by wealthy families. The Greeks liked gold jewelry with intricate patterns and mounted with engraved gems. Drop earrings in the shape of acorns and rosettes, bracelets, anklets and finger rings were also very popular. Men also wore finger rings and, like women, fastened their cloaks with ornate metal brooches.

Much of the silver came from the mines at Laurium, near Athens, where rich veins of silver were discovered in the early fifth century B.C.

Silver coin showing the fine work of a silversmith

The city-state of Athens leased the mines to various syndicates who used slave gangs working up to 10 hours a day. The profits were enormous. One politician, Nicias, profited by supplying his gang of 1,000 slaves for labor. The tunnels, about 90 m below the ground, were so small the miners must have crawled along on their stomachs. Materials were carried by children not yet in their teens and slaves were chained on the surface of the mine to prevent escapes.

Mine at Laurium

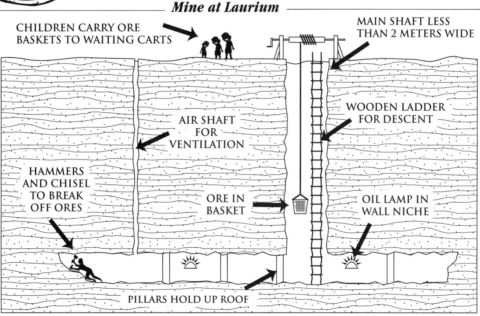

CHILDREN CARRY ORE BASKETS TO WAITING CARTS

MAIN SHAFT LESS THAN 2 METERS WIDE

AIR SHAFT FOR VENTILATION

WOODEN LADDER FOR DESCENT

HAMMERS AND CHISEL TO BREAK OFF ORES

ORE IN BASKET

OIL LAMP IN WALL NICHE

PILLARS HOLD UP ROOF

Activity Box

1. Draw a detailed diagram of your own design for a drop earring, coin, or finger ring. If you want to draw a coin design you could use the owl, the symbol for Athens seen on Athenian coins.

2. Imagine you are a silver miner, a slave working many meters below the ground in terrible conditions. Think of the dust, the dangers, long hours of backbreaking work and your family back home in your own country. On another piece of paper, describe how you feel about your present life and how you would like to change it.

ARTS AND CRAFTS (4)

Teacher's Notes

The earliest glass-makers were from Mesopotamia (now Iraq). They discovered how to make glass with a melted mixture of soda, lime and sand. Glass was valued highly by the Greeks because it resembled precious stones when colored with different minerals.

After the fifth century B.C., statues were created to honor important people like famous writers (Homer), politicians (Pericles), and philosophers (Socrates).

Sculptors in later years paid more attention to details in the human body and in clothing as in the famous Venus de Milo statue found on the island of Milos.

Much of our knowledge of Athenian sculpture comes from unearthed relief gravestones and through their burial of marble sculptures from the Acropolis when the Greeks decided not to rebuild their temples which were demolished by the Persians when they sacked Athens.

Two brilliant sculptors of the Classical Age (ca. 500–300 B.C.) were Pheidias in Athens and Polyclitus from Argos. Pheidias designed the sculptures on the Parthenon in Athens and some of these—about 50—are now in the British Museum. There are people in many countries who believe they should be returned to Greece.

ARTS AND CRAFTS (4)

By the second century B.C., Greek glassworkers were producing vases, bowls, jewelry and perfume jars for holding scented oils. They knew how to make clear glass so they made articles using clear and colored glass together as they looked more attractive. Some glass bowls were made using a method known as the "slumping process." In this process, strips of clear and colored glass were heated and laid on top of each other. They were then rolled up until they resembled a Swiss roll. While still soft, the "roll" was sliced up into sections which were then placed together in the flat, circular shape of the bowl. This was then heated further until the sections melted together. When cool, the flat shape was placed on top of a clay mold in a kiln where the heat caused the flat shape to sag down over the mold to form a bowl.

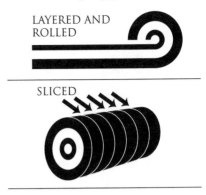

LAYERED AND ROLLED

SLICED

SLICES MELTED TOGETHER

In Ancient Greece, art was for the people and sculptors worked in stone, marble and bronze to produce superb statues which were displayed in temples, public places and Greek homes. Statues usually represented gods and goddesses, victorious athletes, famous Greeks, or heroes and heroines of Greek legends. Some statues had work by other craftsmen—copper lips, glass amber eyes and silver teeth! Sculptors aimed to make statues lifelike, especially male figures, so later years saw more natural poses. Statues were also sculpted in wood, but wooden statues have long disappeared and we are aware of them only through writings of that era.

Statue of Asclepius, the Greek god of medicine

FLAT BOWL

SAGS   CLAY MOLD   SAGS IN HOT KILN

Activity Box

Use the grid squares to make this bust of Solon **twice as big**. Solon was a famous Greek elected as an "archon" (an important magistrate) in 594 B.C.

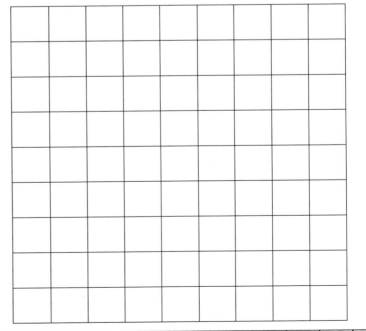

ARTS AND CRAFTS (5)

Teacher's Notes

Wooden dining couches were the main items of furniture, especially in the homes of rich Greeks. Any wooden front door made by a carpenter belonged to the owner, not the house.

Virtually no remains of leather or wooden items have been found for they have rotted away over the years. We know about them from written descriptions and vase and wall paintings.

Fresco painting on wet plaster was permanent as the colors bonded with the plaster. Tempera paints were made using coloring matter from plants and mineral ores. They were ground into a powder and mixed with honey to prevent them from drying quickly and egg white to help the paint to stick to the surface. "Encaustic" artwork was warmed until the colors merged and was used on coffins and wooden panels.

Additional Activity

1. Do your own encaustic painting by mixing wax crayons and candle wax scrapings which can be melted in the sun or in a microwave oven. The paint can be applied with a flexible piece of metal or plastic (Greek artists used knives).

   "Encaustic" comes from the Greek "en" (in) + "kaiein" (to burn).

2. Make your own mosaic panel.

   (a) Ask an adult/teacher to break up colored ceramic tiles/plates inside a couple of strong plastic bags using a hammer. (Discontinued tiles can be obtained free or cheaply from tile retailers).

   (b) Use the shallow lid of an old plastic lunch box or cardboard box.

   (c) Spread soft modeling clay over the lid or mix some cement/plaster of Paris into a thick consistency (one part cement, three parts sand and one part water).

   (d) Partly press broken crockery/tiles into the plaster/cement and design a pattern or picture.

ARTS AND CRAFTS (5)

Basket for storing wool

Other craftsmen like carpenters made plain wooden furniture for ordinary Greek homes or more ornate tables and chairs inlaid with ivory for the rich. Leather workers made belts and sandals for men and women as well as leather shields and breast plates for Greek soldiers. Apart from women in the home, professional weavers wove wall hangings and basket makers sold their wares in the market.

The Greeks appeared to enjoy color and painted stone carvings on temples, gravestones and statues, though artists of the Classical Age seemed to work in only four colors. Artists used different painting techniques—colors mixed with water and painted on wet plaster or the use of tempera paints on house walls.

The mosaic shows a Greek farmer plowing his land and guiding his oxen. His simple plow was a pointed piece of timber tipped with metal which made a furrow but didn't turn over the soil. Later plows had wheels.

In "encaustic" painting, which didn't wash off, colors were mixed with beeswax and plant resins and kept hot while the artists worked.

Using small, fired clay tiles, the Greeks made pictures of everyday life to decorate their walls and floors.

Activity Box

Complete the crossword puzzle. All answers are found in the five pages on "Arts and Crafts."

Across

1. They sold their wares in the market (agora)
2. Engraved and used on jewelry
3. Cloak fasteners
5. World's first ironworkers lived near this sea
7. Slaves worked up to _____ hours a day
9. Wine storage jar
11. Less of this makes bronze stronger
12. Household item made of fired clay
13. Jewelry item
14. Mixed with colors in paint
15. Found at Laurium
18. Used in furnaces

Down

1. Stored in baskets
2. Popular for jewelry
3. Mixed with colors
4. Used to make bronze
6. Used to fire clay
8. Wall pictures made from tiles
9. The best Greek pottery came from here
10. Represented legendary heroes
16. Needed high temperatures to melt
17. A metal is obtained from this

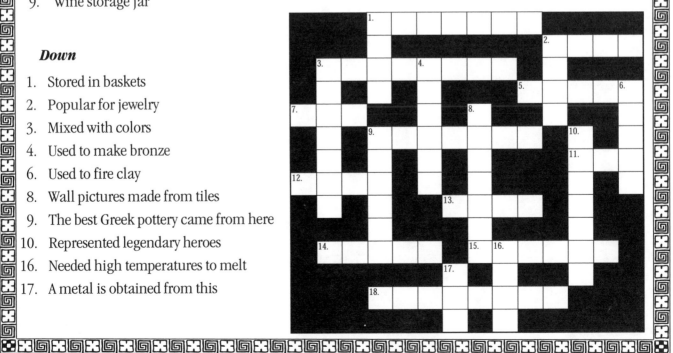

THE OLYMPIC GAMES (1)

Teacher's Notes

Over the years, the original Olympia site was flooded and covered by landslides until it was discovered by Englishman Richard Chandler in 1766. However, it wasn't until 1876 that a German team (guided to the area because local inhabitants raided the site for building stone) excavated thousands of bronze victory offerings and many statues and other sculptures.

There were other sporting festivals: the Pythian (every 4 years), the Isthmian and the Nemean (each every 2 years) where winners wore crowns of laurel leaves, pine needles, parsley, or celery. None of these matched the importance of the Games at Olympia. The Panathenaic Games, to honor the goddess Athene, were held in Athens for Athenians only and victors were presented with a vase containing olive oil.

During the Olympic religious ceremony, animals would be sacrificed. On the opening day, all athletes swore an oath that they were freeborn Greeks and would not cheat.

In the spring of an Olympic year, three "sacred heralds" traveled around Hellas (Greece) reminding competitors to arrive one month before the announced date of the opening ceremony. They could then train before the judges who wore purple robes and could punish athletes disobeying training rules, committing fouls, or accepting bribes, by fines, flogging, or even exclusion from the games. Latecomers to training needed a valid excuse such as pirate attack, shipwreck, or illness.

It is almost certain that the long jump was a kind of multiple jump, because the recorded distances, around 16.5 meters, are much longer than modern long jump records.

THE OLYMPIC GAMES (1)

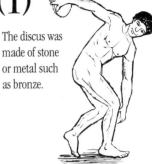

The discus was made of stone or metal such as bronze.

The first ancient Olympic Games is believed to have been held at the foot of Mt. Kronos near Olympia in 776 B.C. in honor of Zeus, father of the gods, for the site had been a shrine to Zeus since 1000 B.C. Olympia was not an ancient Greek city, but a holy place on the west coast of the Peloponnesian peninsula. From around 572 B.C., the games were controlled at Olympia by the city of Elis, in a district of the same name. The single-day religious festival with only one, then two or three races, watched by thousands, gradually became five-day games with tens of thousands of spectators.

The sporting contests were held in July every four years (an olympiad) until they were banned around 390 A.D. by the Roman emperor Theodosius, for they were no longer held in high regard because of growing corruption. They were revived in 1896 in Athens by Baron Pierre de Coubertin, despite opposition in his native France where the emphasis in secondary schools was placed on intellectual studies rather than games or physical training. The modern games have been held every four years in various parts of the world unless interrupted by war.

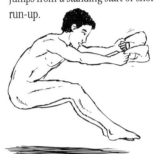

Long jump athletes used stone or metal weights to lengthen their jumps from a standing start or short run-up.

Athletes in the ancient games were amateurs, mainly wealthy Greeks who could afford the money and time to train. They had to be free men who did not represent any city but entered as individuals, and who were barefoot and naked when they competed. Competitors came from all over Greece and from Greek colonies around the Mediterranean. Slaves and foreigners could not compete but were allowed to watch the games.

The first event in the ancient games, the 200 m.

There was only the 200 m race (the "stadion") in the early years, and it wasn't until 724 B.C. that a second race, the 400 m, was included. Gradually, over many years, discus and javelin throws, longer foot races (but no marathon), long jump, wrestling, chariot races, boxing events for boys and races in armor were introduced.

Activity Box

1. How many years passed before Elis controlled the games?

   _____

2. The ancient games began as a religious festival. True or False?

   _____

3. When are the modern games not held?

   _____

4. How many sporting events were held in the games in 776 B.C?

   _____

5. Why did a Roman emperor ban the ancient games?

   _____

6. Who was worshipped at the shrine at Olympia?

   _____

7. What is the period between the games known as?

   _____

8. Why was there opposition in France to Coubertin's revival of modern sporting games?

   _____

THE OLYMPIC GAMES (2)

Teacher's Notes

The first boys' events were the 200-meter sprint and wrestling, both introduced in 632 B.C. A boy from Elis won the race and a Spartan boy the wrestling. Any male between the ages of 12 and 18 was regarded as a boy.

The huge statue of Zeus in his temple at Olympia was made of gold and ivory in the later years of the fifth century B.C. It was made by the great sculptor Pheidias and was recognized as one of the ancient Seven Wonders of the World.

Swimming and the high jump were never events in the ancient games.

In 512 B.C., one man won the 200 m, the 400 m and the race in armor on the same day, the first triple winner in the ancient games.

The word "pankration" comes from the Greek adjective "pankrates" which means "all-powerful."

Bribery scandals have been part of the modern Olympics, but the first recorded one was in 388 B.C., when a boxer was fined and banned from the games for bribing two of his opponents to lose their fights.

Not all Greeks liked the games, and when a victor boasted that he was the fastest runner in all Greece, the famous philosopher Diogenes said,

"But not faster than a rabbit or a deer, and they, the swiftest of the animals, are also the most cowardly."

Additional Activity

Work in groups to make a list of what you consider are the Seven Wonders of the Modern World, then report to the class so a class decision could be made.

THE OLYMPIC GAMES (2)

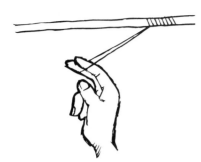

Finger thong as shown on Greek vases

The best athletes usually entered the five events called the pentathlon, which was introduced to the games in 708 B.C. The pentathlon included the 200 m, javelin throw, discus, long jump and wrestling. The javelin was a slim length of sharpened wood, usually from the elder tree. It had a small hurling thong attached and this helped to rotate the shaft to increase the distance and keep its flight straight. The runners had a starting line of marble stones against which the athlete placed his back foot, but simple starting gates for foot races were introduced around 450 B.C. In boxing there were no rounds or rules, with the last man still on his feet crowned as the winner. Gloves were not used until 4 B.C. In wrestling, biting was not allowed but it was all right to break an opponent's fingers!

The "pankration," introduced in 648 B.C., was a combination of boxing and wrestling for tough athletes in which eye gouging and biting were illegal. It continued until one antagonist surrendered by tapping the victor on the back or shoulder. The event was described by a poet named Xenophanes as "that new and terrible contest," for there were occasional fatalities—but it was still a very popular event with spectators.

Zeus on a silver 350 B.C. coin from Elis, probably associated with Olympic festivals

The victor receives his crown of olive leaves.

After it was introduced at Olympia in 520 B.C., the final sporting event was the armor race. It was a gruelling event in which the athletes wore heavy body armor as they ran 400 m in the Olympic stadium, which was almost 200 m long and covered in sand.

Activity Box

Imagine you are a reporter. Write a short sports report on what you imagine the event called the Pankration would have been like.

_____

_____

_____

_____

_____

_____

_____

_____

_____

_____

_____

THE OLYMPIC GAMES (3)

Teacher's Notes

For 200 years after 776 B.C., there were no stone buildings or temples at Olympia (the Temple of Zeus wasn't built until after 500 B.C.), only earth embankments for spectators and a handful of seats, some made of marble, for important visitors.

Apart from spectators, people at the games included food and drink vendors, city representatives bearing gifts for Zeus, gamblers, flower sellers and singers, dancers and orators providing entertainment.

The rewards for winning athletes could be a pension for life, or free food for the rest of their days, or freedom from paying taxes. Victors, who in the early years came mainly from the Greek mainland, were praised in poetry and song. The first winner was a cook called Koroibos.

Only quality records were kept—the boxers who were "never wounded" or the wrestlers never brought to their knees.

Trainers looked after the welfare of the athletes and no doctors were present at the games before the third century A.D.

As in modern times, the ancient games at Olympia were affected by wars, such as the invasion by Sparta in 400 B.C., and trouble with neighbors Arcadia in 364 B.C., when the pentathlon was interrupted.

An ancient tale is told of a widow in 404 B.C. wanting to watch her son in the boys' boxing event. She disguised herself as a male trainer but, in her excitement, when her son won, she leapt over a barrier and accidentally revealed she was a women. A rule was then introduced to ensure trainers were also naked.

Additional Activity

What do you think of the ban on women as spectators—was it a practical one (because male athletes were nude) or did it reflect the ancient Greek society's attitude towards women?

Ancient Greece

THE OLYMPIC GAMES (3)

Crowds up to 40,000 are believed to have watched the ancient games, and throughout their history, all spectators were admitted without charge. Women could not watch or compete in the games at Olympia but married women had their own games dedicated to goddesses such as Hera or Demeter. It wasn't until a later time when Greece (Hellas) was a part of the Roman Empire that women were allowed to the games as spectators and later as competitors. By that time, naked athletes were no longer allowed.

Two types of long jump weights.

Strigil (Scraper)
All athletes covered their bodies with oil as protection and to loosen muscles. After an event, the oil, along with the dust, was scraped off with this metal tool called a strigil. Athletes also sponged themselves down and then applied perfume to refresh their bodies.

Only the winners were presented with a crown of olive leaves from a sacred olive tree near the later temple of Zeus, a tree believed to give magical powers. However, the victors could expect other rewards when they returned to a proud home city.

There was no timing for records and no medals of gold, silver, or bronze. Judges, who carried whips to maintain discipline and prevent cheating, were responsible to an Olympic Council.

Later games lasted five days with religious ceremonies and sacrifices to Zeus on the first day, while a parade of victors and a banquet in the Magistrates' house on the last day ended the games.

Broken tombstone of a gymnasiarch (official in charge of a gymnasium). It shows a wreath, three tablets with portraits, an ax, three strigils, two palm trees and an oil tank with three ladles for athletes to use.

Activity Box

1. Hold a standing long jump group competition in the playground. Present the winner in each group with a crown of leaves!

2. In groups, discuss the differences and the similarities between the ancient and modern games. Report to the class so the class result can be shown on the board.

Similarities	Differences
Thousands watched both games.	No high jump in ancient games.

GODS AND GODDESSES (1)

Teacher's Notes

The usual animal sacrifices were pigs, sheep, goats, or even poultry, with oxen for special ceremonies. The communal eating of the meat afterwards was an important part of the ceremony.

Individual gods had their own priests, but the priests had no training or qualifications for it was generally a part-time occupation.

By 395 B.C., the Roman emperor Theodosius had banned pagan rites at a time when many Greeks had turned to Christianity.

The people of Elis built the temple of Zeus at Olympia out of local limestone, using the services of an architect called Libon. They then asked Pheidias, the most famous and acclaimed sculptor of the century, to make his huge statue. The remains of the sculptor's workshop have been found as well as, in the ruins, a pottery cup with his name scratched on the surface. Critics of that time have criticized the proportions of the statue in relation to the temple's size, saying that if the god stood up his head would go through the roof!

Ambrosia was thought to be carried by pigeons to Zeus who sent it to the other gods. Mortals permitted to eat it were supposed to gain in beauty, strength and speed and become immortal.

In Greek myths, the gods had a fluid called "ichor" flowing through their veins instead of blood.

GODS AND GODDESSES (1)

The Greeks worshipped dozens of gods and goddesses. They believed they were immortal and that they watched over all aspects of their lives. The most important and most powerful gods were the 12 Olympians (the Pantheon) who lived on Mount Olympus, the highest mountain in Greece. This group of 12 was recognized from the fifth century B.C. Like the writer Homer, the Greeks thought their gods were like humans, as they married, had children, quarreled among themselves, and had human failings like jealousy and anger. However, they also thought that only the gods and goddesses had the power to control a person's fate. The gods ate special food called ambrosia and drank nectar as they dealt with the lives of ordinary mortals on Earth. Prayers to the gods on Mount Olympus were offered with hands in the air, whereas prayers to gods of the underworld were recited with hands lowered. If people wanted a special favor from the gods, they would sacrifice an animal at an outside shrine or altar. Worship took place outside a temple, which was regarded as the home of the god. Though the Olympian gods and goddesses were worshipped all over Greece, some had special links with particular places or regions, like Athena with the city of Athens.

This statue of Zeus in gold and ivory was regarded as one of the Seven Wonders of the World at that time. It was made by Pheidias, one of the greatest of the Greek sculptors, in the latter part of the fifth century B.C. The statue was 12 meters high and placed in the inner chamber of the temple of Zeus.

Activity Box

1. Color in the statue of Zeus on his throne. Remember it was made of gold and ivory.

2. List the characteristics believed to be possessed by the gods, under the following headings.

Human-like	Not Human-like

GODS AND GODDESSES (2)

Teacher's Notes

Zeus: Ruler of the gods and controller of the sky, storms, thunder and lightning. Married to his sister Hera and other goddesses. His symbols were the thunderbolt, eagle and oak tree. A calendar from Attica described him as "kindly Zeus" and "Zeus who looks after men," just two of hundreds of descriptions of him. He took power by overthrowing the Titans, giants in Greek mythology.

Hestia: Goddess of the home. Every Greek city and family had a shrine dedicated to her and there was one in the Magistrates' House at Olympia. She was gentle and avoided arguments among the gods. When Zeus declared that Dionysos, the god of wine, should have a place on Olympus, Hestia left the home of the gods so there would not be an unlucky 13 gods.

Demeter: The goddess of agriculture and all plants, especially corn. The Greeks thought winter was the time when Demeter neglected plants and searched for her daughter Persephone, kidnapped by her uncle, Hades. Her symbols were a sheaf of wheat or barley.

Ares: The god of war and the son of Zeus and Hera. He was quick-tempered and violent and his symbols were a burning torch, a spear, dogs and vultures.

Poseidon: Ruler of the seas and brother of Zeus. Lived in an underwater palace with white horses and a gold chariot. Believed to cause earthquakes and storms at sea so sailors made offerings to him if they returned safely. His symbols were horses, dolphins and a trident, a three-pronged spear which was the symbol of fishermen. He was the father of legendary Athenian hero Theseus who slew the minotaur, a beast half man and half bull.

Aphrodite: Goddess of love and beauty who was born in the sea and sailed to shore in Cyprus on a scallop shell. She wore a belt of gold and, though married, loved Ares. Nobody knew who her parents were though in Homer's writings she was the daughter of Zeus. Her symbols were roses, sparrows, dolphins and rams.

Hera: Wife of Zeus and protector of women and marriage. She was beautiful and proud and resented her husband's affairs with mortal women. The head of this goddess, probably from her temple at Olympia, has been unearthed and appears to be of Spartan style. Games were held in her honor at Argos. Her symbols were the peacock and pomegranate.

Hades: Brother of Zeus and ruler of the underworld, the realms of the dead whom he rarely allowed to return to Earth. He also had the name Pluto in Greek and Roman myths. He owned all the gems and precious metals in the ground.

GODS AND GODDESSES (2)

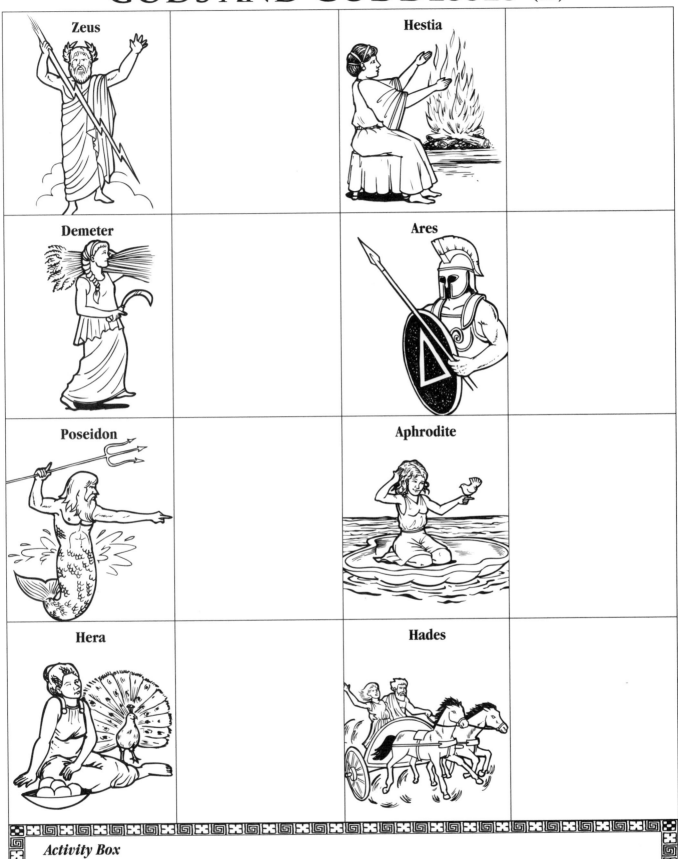

Zeus

Hestia

Demeter

Ares

Poseidon

Aphrodite

Hera

Hades

Activity Box

Listen to or read the information provided by the teacher. Then list words to describe each god/goddess in the boxes.

ATHENS AND SPARTA

Teacher's Notes

The Peloponnese Peninsula was named after a mythical king called Pelops. Spartan soldiers culled the helots each year to maintain their warrior image.

To maintain high standards of physical health in order to give birth to fine warriors, Spartan girls even performed physical activities in public, which highly offended Athenians who thought it was improper behavior. Though Spartan women enjoyed more freedom from domestic chores and more favorable property rights than Athenian women, they suffered from bans on jewelry, cosmetics, perfume and colored clothing.

The Delian League was so called because its headquarters were on the island of Delos; it was virtually an Athenian empire.

In 464 B.C., Sparta suffered a violent earthquake and when some Spartan subjects rebelled, Sparta asked its allies for help. Athens sent 4,000 soldiers, but the Spartans distrusted the Athenians so much they sent them back, an insult to the city of Athens.

Alexander the Great, who had conquered the Greek mainland, died in 323 B.C. and neither Athens nor Sparta ever again controlled the other city-states, though Athens was still celebrated for its culture. Sparta today is a modern provincial town with few reminders of its past, whereas Athens is renowned for its magnificent architecture from a glorious bygone age.

ATHENS AND SPARTA

A thens became the largest, most prosperous city-state while Sparta, the main Dorian settlement and capital of Laconia, controlled southern Greece, known as the Peloponnese. Each was an independent state and, though they had the same gods and language, they were rivals for many years. Sparta was ruled by two jointly reigning kings who had no real power except as military leaders, for Spartans were controlled by a small group of nobles (an oligarchy) who ruled their subjects and helots (slaves).

Athens was more democratic, with ordinary citizens having a bigger say in government policy and lawmaking though, like Sparta, citizenship was granted to a limited range of the population.

In Greece, children were important in order to care for aged parents as there were no pensions. Even so, children in Sparta who were found to be sickly or handicapped after inspection by tribal elders, were left to die or were thrown over a cliff. This differed from Athens, where emphasis was on the family.

When the Persian invaders were defeated in 479 B.C., with Sparta victorious on land and Athens at sea, the same old problem of who was the prominent power in Greece arose. As a result, in 478 B.C., Athens formed the Delian League, a power group of most city-states, islands and colonies in the eastern Mediterranean, which developed into an Athenian empire.

When the great statesman Pericles became leader of Athens in 460 B.C., he led the Athenians, with the help of taxes from the members of the Delian League, into a period known as the "Golden Age." But the Spartans did not accept his vision of Athens as capital of all Greece. The formation of the Delian League had angered Sparta's Peloponnesian League, supported by Corinth and Thebes, especially when Athens seemed to be planning to extend its Empire into the western Mediterranean.

Pericles

Activity Box

1. What name is given to "rule by a few"? _____

2. Which city-state had the stronger army, Athens or Sparta? _____

3. Name one way in which Athens and Sparta were similar.

   _____

4. Which phrase tells us their struggle for power had lasted many years?

   _____

5. How did Spartan society treat its sickly or handicapped children?

   _____

   _____

PELOPONNESIAN WARS

Teacher's Notes

During the 2nd Peloponnesian War, battles were on a huge scale and the armies included foot soldiers (hoplites) with their heavy and expensive armor, new lightly-armed troops (peltasts) and cavalry. Sea warfare and siege methods also developed more quickly.

Sparta was also worried about Athenian westward expansion, because their corn supplies came from the Greek colonies in Sicily.

During the war years, Sparta invaded Attica, the region around Athens, five times, destroying crops and cutting down olive trees, which took 15 years to grow, as well as grapevines.

The Athenian plan was to attack Sparta by sea and deny the Spartans the chance of using their superior soldiers in land battles.

The true Spartans, the Spartiates, had to be permanently prepared for war, and any Spartan soldier not considered brave enough was made to grow only half a beard so he would be recognized.

Thousands of captured Athenians worked in the huge stone quarries in the old Greek colony of Syracuse in Sicily. The quarries are still there today. The attack on Sicily was the worst defeat in the history of Athens.

At the end of the war in 404 B.C., the Spartans abolished democracy in Athens and replaced it with an oligarchy known as the "thirty tyrants," but the Athenians rebelled and reinstated democracy after only 12 months. The Greek city-states were pleased to be free from control by Athens, but the Spartans were now harsh masters. Spartan domination didn't last long and soon Thebes became the new powerful city-state, though Athens did regain its prosperity.

The Athenians began to rebuild their long walls in 395 B.C.

Additional Activity

Use reference sources and write a few of your own sentences about Lysander, the Spartan General, who is mentioned in the song "The British Grenadiers."

PELOPONNESIAN WARS

Spartan warrior

Horse hair crest

Body armor (cuirass); metal strips with leather backing or glued linen strips

Bronze shield (a hopla)

Iron-tipped stabbing spear

Cloak dyed red to hide any blood

Iron sword

Greaves for protecting the legs

After years of rivalry and the first Peloponnesian War (ca. 460–446 B.C.) between Sparta and Athens, several city-states and Corinth asked for Sparta's help. They wanted to stop Athenian plans to extend their Empire westwards, so Sparta declared war on Athens in 431 B.C.

This fierce struggle for power continued, with one short period of peace, for 27 years. It was the Second or Great Peloponnesian War.

Bronze statue of a Spartan warrior ca. 500 B.C.

The Athenian leader, Pericles, persuaded the Assembly to order their citizens in Attica to leave their homes and shelter behind the defensive walls around Athens. Huge numbers—around 150,000—now populated the city, and plague brought in by the Athenian grain ships broke out in 429 B.C. in the overcrowded capital, killing thousands, including the great Athenian leader, Pericles, who lingered for six months before dying.

While Sparta had Greece's strongest army, having already conquered its neighboring states, Athens had the most powerful navy and commanded the seas. So, although armies laid waste to the region around Athens, they couldn't prevent the city's supplies coming by sea. In 413 B.C., Athens made a foolish attack on Sicily and was heavily defeated, losing 200 warships and 50,000 troops were killed or taken prisoner.

A few years later, Persian gold helped Sparta build a fleet, and a great Spartan general, Lysander, defeated the Athenian navy at the Dardanelles in the eastern Mediterranean. He then sailed for Piraeus, the port of Athens, with about 150 ships. He blocked off the grain supplies from south Russia so the Athenians were forced to surrender, and in 404 B.C. the war ended. The Corinthians demanded the traditional practice of killing all the men and selling the women and children into slavery. However, Sparta abolished the Delian League, destroyed the Athenian navy (restricting their fleet to only 12 ships), and made the Athenians pull down the Long Walls, defensive walls which had stood for 50 years.

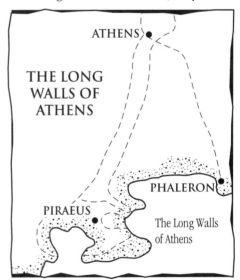

THE LONG WALLS OF ATHENS

ATHENS

PHALERON

PIRAEUS

The Long Walls of Athens

Activity Box

1. What events occurred in the following years:

   (a) 431 B.C. _____

   (b) 429 B.C. _____

   (c) 413 B.C. _____

   (d) 404 B.C. _____

AT WAR

Teacher's Notes

Hoplites put their armor on last as it was very heavy and their helmets often restricted their hearing and vision. Their round shields were also heavy and were tied to the arm in several places to prevent them being snatched away by the enemy.

Hoplites in phalanxes from Thebes had spears up to six meters long, a similar length to the later reorganized Macedonian phalanx, in which the shorter throwing spear was replaced by a longer thrusting pike.

The Spartan poet, Tyrtaeus, wrote that the function of the phalanx was to "stand near and take the enemy, strike with long spear or sword, set foot by foot, lean shield on shield, crest upon crest, helmet on helmet . . ."

Helmets often had decorative, detachable feathers and Corinthian-style helmets were lined with soft leather or fabric.

Most Greek troops fought on foot, but a wealthy soldier from a landowning family was expected to provide himself with a horse as well as armor and weapons, unless his father had died in battle. War orphans in Athens were given public financial support. There was no need for complex arrangements for the transportation of equipment and supplies as in modern warfare, for troops provided their own food and equipment. Some of those who couldn't provide weapons served as oarsmen on Greek warships.

Like many of their army and navy leaders, Greek soldiers weren't experts in military tactics, but by discipline and enthusiasm tried to emulate the heroic deeds of legendary heroes from their ancient myths.

Additional Activity

Make a Corinthian helmet/own helmet from papier-mâché around an upturned bowl.

Make a round hoplite shield with center decoration from cardboard.

Some shield designs on Greek pottery

Ancient Greece

AT WAR

Greek Phalanx

Much of our information about Greek soldiers comes from written descriptions, pictures of Greeks at war on painted pottery and from discarded shields, weapons and armor found in large numbers of filled-in wells at Olympia. Though the Greeks could make iron, during the Peloponnesian wars many shields, weapons and breastplates were still being made of bronze.

The main attacking formation was the phalanx, a square arrangement of foot soldiers (hoplites) armed with spears around 3 to 4 meters in length. The leading troops would hold their spears horizontally to present a moving front of spear points to the enemy, while the rear rows held their spears up to deflect enemy missiles. This formation was very effective in blocking a road or narrow mountain pass.

Cavalry was sometimes used to protect an army's flanks or pursue fleeing enemy troops, but the mountainous terrain in Greece was not suitable for chariots when the city-states fought each other.

A Corinthian helmet from the city-state of Corinth. Each region had a helmet of a different shape.

When soldiers were needed for battle, ordinary citizens made up the armies, which were led by aristocrats from wealthy families. Poor farmers or craftsmen used slings or bows while men who could afford armor became hoplites. Though the custom changed in later years, battles were usually fought in the summer months, the "fighting season," and during the 2nd Peloponnesian War fighting became more savage, with the whole populations of cities being slain or forced into slavery. Between the ages of 18 and 20, citizens became "ephebes" and could be made to do military service for their city-state. Slaves weren't citizens but often served as additional troops called "skirmishers," who protected the flanks of the phalanx with slings for hurling stones or with bows and arrows.

Red-figured vase painting of a warrior leaving his family to fight.

Activity box

1. Why wasn't cavalry very effective in Greek battles?

   _____

   _____

2. What were Greek foot soldiers called?

   _____

3. People who may have to serve in the army or navy were called _____.

4. What do you think the vase shield decoration is?

   _____

5. What thoughts would run through your head if you were facing a phalanx?

   _____

   _____

   _____

   _____

WEAPONS

Teacher's Notes

The Hellenistic era was the period after the death of Alexander the Great in 323 B.C.

In the Archaic period (700–500 B.C.), the common Greek warship was the "penteconter" rowed by 24 oarsmen, but it was too long and narrow and proved to be unseaworthy. The "trireme" replaced the penteconter and the "quinquireme" replaced the trireme after the death of Alexander.

The longest-serving warship in the Mediterranean was the trireme, and at the height of its naval power Athens had 300 triremes, ships developed in Corinth by the best boat builders in the ancient world. According to archaeological evidence, they were about forty meters long and six meters wide. Before a sea battle the crew would sleep ashore, as there was little space aboard the ship for them or the sails. Sails were first used in the Aegean Sea around 2000 B.C. and triremes moved at 4 to 5 knots when under sail.

The captain of a trireme was a "trierarch," often a rich man who would pay the cost of running the ship for a year and be guided by professional sailors.

Experts still differ over the arrangement of oarsmen in the lower deck of a trireme but think this formation was probably the correct one. The ship was steered by a skilled helmsman at the stern of the ship.

a thranite
a zygite
a thalamite (means 'in the hold')

31 rowers in the top level,
27 rowers in the bottom two levels (on each side of the ship)

WEAPONS

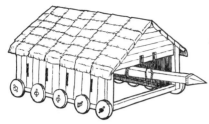

Battering Ram

Mobile battering rams on wheels were used against the walls or gates of enemy cities. The ram, often a tree trunk with a metal point, was suspended on ropes under a protective cover and swung to and fro by a team of men.

Flame thrower

This Hellenistic flame thrower from the fourth century B.C. was used against wooden walls or gates. Huge bellows were worked by a team of men. They forced air through a hollow log and the increased oxygen caused the flames from burning coals in a metal cauldron to flare up and burn the target.

The Catapult

The Greeks invented the catapult around 400 B.C. and, about 50 years later, the torsion catapult, where extra power came from tightly twisted ropes. Early catapults were similar to a crossbow and fired arrows or javelins, not rocks like later versions.

Siege Tower

Siege towers enabled soldiers to scale the walls of besieged cities. Inside were different levels where archers firing arrows or catapults hurling rocks could break the resistance of a defending army. If the besieging army couldn't force a surrender, the siege could last months until starvation made the city's citizens give in.

The Trireme

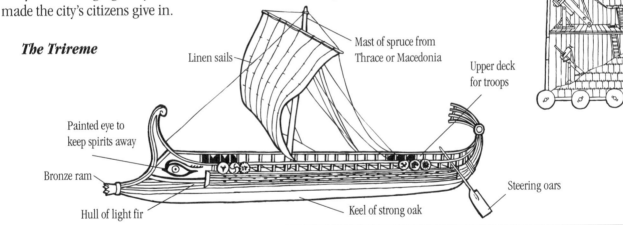

Linen sails

Mast of spruce from Thrace or Macedonia

Upper deck for troops

Painted eye to keep spirits away

Bronze ram

Steering oars

Hull of light fir

Keel of strong oak

Activity Box

Use the given words to complete the passage about the trireme.

cripple	sail	warship	shore	break	enemy	unable	invented
archers	sea	lowered	ships	battle	metal	oarsmen	

In the sixth century B.C. the Greeks _____ [1] the trireme, a fast _____ [2] using about

170 _____ [3] for power. It carried hoplites and _____ [4] who fired arrows at the

_____ [5]. The prow of the ship had a _____ [6] spike under the waterline to _____ [7]

or sink enemy _____ [8], or to _____ [9] their oars so they were _____ [10]

to maneuver. The trireme carried a _____ [11] for use in the open _____ [12] but this

was _____ [13] or left on the _____ [14] before a _____ [15] commenced.

THE PERSIAN WARS (1)

Teacher's Notes

The Greek colonies were in what is now Turkey.

The strength of the Persian armies was built on their key soldiers, the archers, who showered swarms of arrows onto opposing troops before the enemy could use their spears or swords in hand-to-hand fighting.

Darius sent ambassadors to the Greek city-states demanding that he be accepted as their ruler but, though some agreed, Athens and Sparta killed the messengers.

Before the battle of Marathon, the Greek general, Miltiades, sent athlete Pheidippides to seek help from Sparta. After running for two days and two nights and a distance over 200 km he returned, fought in the battle, then ran 42 km to Athens with news of the victory—before dropping dead. The Olympic marathon race remembers this remarkable feat.

After the battle the dead Athenians were buried in a common grave. The burial mound can still be seen in Greece today.

Still fearing the Persians after the battle of Marathon, the command of Greek armies was given to the Spartans and the Athenians began to build up a strong navy.

Ancient Greece

THE PERSIAN WARS (1)

Cyrus the Great

Persian soldier

The Persians and Greeks were long-time enemies. Greek colonies had been founded on the eastern shores of the Aegean Sea since about 1050 B.C. Around 546 B.C., the colonies of Ionia and Lydia became part of the powerful Persian Empire when conquered by Cyrus the Great, king of Persia, who founded the Empire. Cyrus then used the gold from Lydia's mines to pay for his military campaigns.

A later Persian king, Darius I, forced the Ionian colonies to pay taxes and serve in the Persian armies, so the Greek colonies, with help from Athens and other city-states, rebelled in 499 B.C. and destroyed the Persian city of Sardis. After the mainland Greeks returned home, Darius defeated the rebels in 494 B.C. and burned down Miletus, an important Ionian town. Darius then sent a huge army in 600 ships to punish Athens for assisting the colonies and killing his ambassadors, who had been sent to advise surrender. However, in 490 B.C., the Athenians won a great victory on the plains of Marathon against a Persian army many times bigger than the 10,000 hoplites. The Persians fled to their ships after losing 6,400 men, whereas the Greeks lost fewer than 200 troops.

This was the first major military defeat suffered by armies of the Persian Empire.

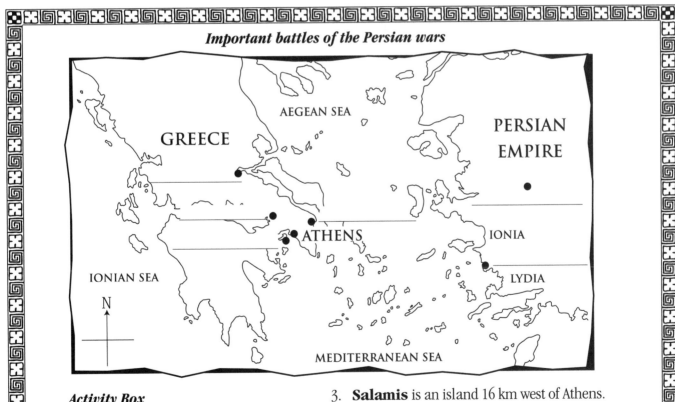

Important battles of the Persian wars

AEGEAN SEA

GREECE

PERSIAN EMPIRE

ATHENS

IONIA

IONIAN SEA

LYDIA

N

MEDITERRANEAN SEA

Activity Box

Complete the map using the clues below

1. **Sardis** is the most eastern town.

2. **Miletus** is southwest of Sardis.

3. **Salamis** is an island 16 km west of Athens.

4. **Marathon** is northeast of Athens.

5. **Thermopylae** is northwest of Plataea.

6. **Plataea** is southeast of Thermopylae.

THE PERSIAN WARS (2)

Teacher's Notes

To stabilize the bridge of boats, ropes were tied to heavy rocks which were then lowered to the seabed. Planks were laid across the boats and covered with straw and soil so men, horses and carts could cross.

After the destruction of Athens by the Persians, the Athenians recaptured their city but left some damaged property unrepaired for many years as a memorial to those citizens who died fighting the Persians.

The orders for the evacuation of Athens, engraved on a stone tablet for public display, have been found in the back of a Greek coffee house.

The Persians weren't a seafaring nation and, in sea battles, used Phoenician and Egyptian warships and sailors against the Greeks.

In the battle of Salamis, the Athenian triremes were smaller and much more maneuverable than the enemy warships. Xerxes watched the battle from Mount Aegaleus and saw his fleet routed by the Greeks, who destroyed or disabled over 200 Persian ships. Many Persian soldiers drowned as they couldn't swim like the Greeks.

Following the defeat of the Persians, the Greeks enjoyed almost 50 years of peace.

Ancient Greece

THE PERSIAN WARS (2)

In 480 B.C., Xerxes, the son of Darius, who died in 486 B.C., led a huge army into Greece, determined to beat the old enemy. He crossed the Hellespont, a narrow stretch of water between Asia and Europe about 1.5 km wide, by building a bridge of boats held in place by ropes. His army defeated the Spartans, under Leonidas, at Thermopylae, where 300 Spartans and some Thebans defended a narrow mountain pass. The defending soldiers were attacked from the rear along a poorly guarded mountain track and the Thebans surrendered, but all the Spartans died, fighting fiercely to the end. Xerxes then marched on to Athens so the Athenian general, Themistocles, who fought at Marathon, evacuated all women and children to the Greek islands off the coast and left only a few soldiers to

defend Athens. The Persians overran the city and destroyed most of the temples, public buildings, statues and monuments. Themistocles then led his fleet of about 300 triremes into the most important battle of the Persian wars, a sea battle fought off the coast of the island of Salamis, about 16 km west of Athens. He lured the huge Persian fleet of over 1,000 ships into a narrow strait between the island and the mainland and won a brilliant victory. Xerxes returned home and left his troops to finish the campaign, an army larger than the 35,000 soldiers the Greeks could muster. The Greeks defeated his army at Plataea in 479 B.C. and then destroyed the Persian navy in the same year.

Engraved gemstone showing Persian horseman fighting a Greek soldier.

Activity Box

Answer the following questions on the Persian Wars (1 and 2).

1. Who founded the Persian Empire, the largest the world had seen at that time?

_____

2. Why did the Greek colonies rebel?

_____

_____

3. Why were the rebel colonies defeated in 494 B.C.?

_____

4. What was the Persian army's first major defeat?

_____

5. Who was the father of Xerxes?

_____

6. What two actions angered Darius?

_____

_____

7. How many battles (in the notes) were on mainland Greece?

_____

8. Why do you think Cyrus was called "Great"?

_____

_____

9. Why were the Greeks defeated at Thermopylae?

_____

10. What do you think of the plan to build a bridge of boats?

_____

_____

ALEXANDER THE GREAT (1)

The Macedonians were racially and linguistically related to the Greeks. Phillip II so admired the culture of Athens, he appointed the great philosopher Aristotle as his son's tutor. It was Aristotle who taught Alexander, "It is fitting that Greeks should rule barbarians."

Teacher's Notes Alexander put down a revolt in Thebes, then razed the city to the ground—but left temples and the house of Pindar, a famous Greek poet, intact. The residents who survived, about 8,000, were sold as slaves. This severe reprisal had the desired effect and other rebellious city-states negotiated peace.

The Macedonians, under Alexander's father, had adapted the Greek phalanx by extending the sides of the rear lines by about 4.5 meters. They also introduced new cavalry tactics, including formations that attacked the enemy flanks in "wings." They also increased the length of the soldiers' spears.

ALEXANDER THE GREAT (1)

Bronze statue of Alexander during the battle of Granicus.

Alexander was born in 356 B.C. at Pella, the capital city of Macedonia. Mainland Greeks thought Macedonians living outside Hellas (Greece) were only a little better than barbarians and were not true Greeks. Macedonian nobles believed their ancestors were of Greek origin and some tribes spoke Greek. Alexander's father, Philip II, who had conquered most of Greece, was a brilliant soldier and statesman, but he was assassinated at a relative's funeral in 336 B.C. Alexander came to the throne, executed those responsible for his father's death, and then decided to fulfil his father's dream of conquering Persia in revenge for their invasion of Greece 150 years before, though first of all he had to put down revolts by several city-states.

His conquest of the Persian empire took 11 years, and his army of over 50,000 Greeks and Macedonians traveled more than 30,000 km. Alexander's use of the Greek phalanx with mobile, lightly armed infantry and cavalry at the sides won him victory after victory in a long and difficult campaign.

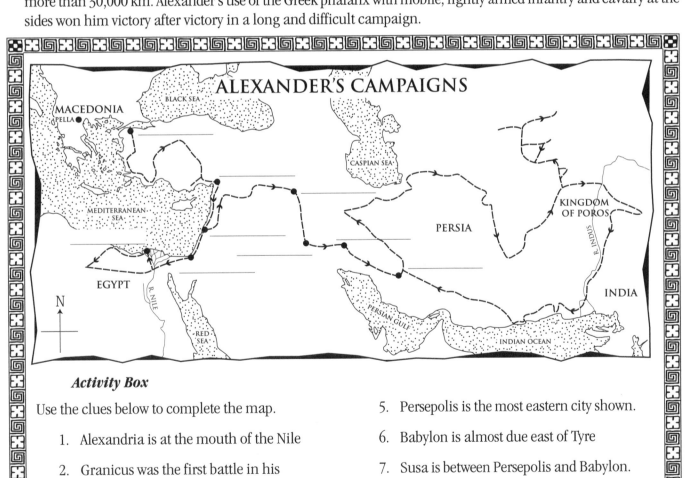

ALEXANDER'S CAMPAIGNS

(map with labels: MACEDONIA, PELLA, BLACK SEA, CASPIAN SEA, MEDITERRANEAN SEA, EGYPT, R. NILE, RED SEA, PERSIAN GULF, PERSIA, KINGDOM OF POROS, R. INDUS, INDIA, INDIAN OCEAN, N)

Activity Box

Use the clues below to complete the map.

1. Alexandria is at the mouth of the Nile

2. Granicus was the first battle in his Persian campaign.

3. Tyre is on the coast west of Babylon.

4. Gaza lies between Tyre and Alexandria.

Check your answers by reading the clues again.

5. Persepolis is the most eastern city shown.

6. Babylon is almost due east of Tyre

7. Susa is between Persepolis and Babylon.

8. Gaugamela is north of Babylon.

9. Issos is west of Gaugemela.

10. The Persian Gulf is south of Persepolis.

ALEXANDER THE GREAT (2)

Teacher's Notes

In his pursuit of Darius, who fled into what is now Afghanistan, half of Alexander's horses perished after traveling over 600 km in fierce heat.

Alexander named scores of cities after himself and even named one Bucephala after his favorite horse, Bucephalus. He ensured the cities were well constructed in the Greek style, had paved roads, were supplied with water and settled with Greeks.

Alexander called Persepolis "the most hated city in the world," and he slaughtered its priests in revenge for the Persian invasion of Greece 150 years before. Today, Athens is a thriving city while Persepolis is a collection of ancient ruins.

Alexander marched on to India with around 60,000 troops, convinced that India was the end of the Earth and he would see the ocean Greeks believed encircled the world. However, his soldiers didn't share his dream of conquering the whole known world of those times, and Alexander is said to have complained, "I have known defeat only from my own soldiers."

Poros's army was routed, but Alexander was so impressed by the rajah's courage, he gave him his kingdom back.

Alexander's shipbuilders constructed over 1,000 ships to sail down the Indus, a voyage which took seven months, with fighting all the way.

Everywhere Alexander traveled in his campaigns, he left behind chosen governors who helped to spread the Greek language and culture over an enormous area of Asia. He encouraged his soldiers to marry Persian brides as he had done when he married the daughter of Darius and later another Persian woman, Roxane.

Alexander left his Empire "to the strongest" and the struggle to succeed him lasted about 50 years, until the Empire was divided into three parts. He also left behind a system of monarchy, for kings had been the traditional rulers of Macedonia.

Additional Activity

Make an accurate drawing of the susa lion made from glazed tiles.

ALEXANDER THE GREAT (2)

Persian war elephant.

After victory at Granicus in Asia Minor (now Turkey) in 334 B.C., Alexander marched south and routed the Persians at Issos the following year. The terrified Persian King, Darius III, fled and left his family behind. Using siege towers and battering rams, Alexander then besieged the Phoenician city of Tyre (in modern Lebanon) for seven months before slaughtering many defending troops and selling women and children into slavery. The fortress at Gaza also surrendered after a long siege. Following the conquest of Egypt, where he was declared a son of God, he moved north and defeated a huge Persian army at Gaugamela (in modern Iraq) in 331 B.C., despite the Persian's use of chariots and war elephants. The following year, Darius was murdered by his own men in a final attempt to save Persia. After breaking all resistance in central Asia, where he sacked Susa and destroyed the Persian capital Persepolis, looting it of its treasures—an act he later regretted— Alexander then moved along the ancient silk trade route into India in 327 B.C. There, he fought against 200 trained war elephants in the army of King Poros and was again successful. Alexander then led his army across the River Indus, but his troops mutinied as they wanted to go home. His men built a fleet of ships and sailed down the Indus. The ships were to sail along the coast to the Persian Gulf and supply food and water to Alexander and his army as they marched westwards across the desert. The ships couldn't sail against the winds and more men were lost through hunger and thirst than in the whole campaign. In 323 B.C., only 32 years old, Alexander died after being ill with fever in Babylon. He was buried in a gold coffin in Egypt.

Decoration on facade of Royal Palace at Susa.

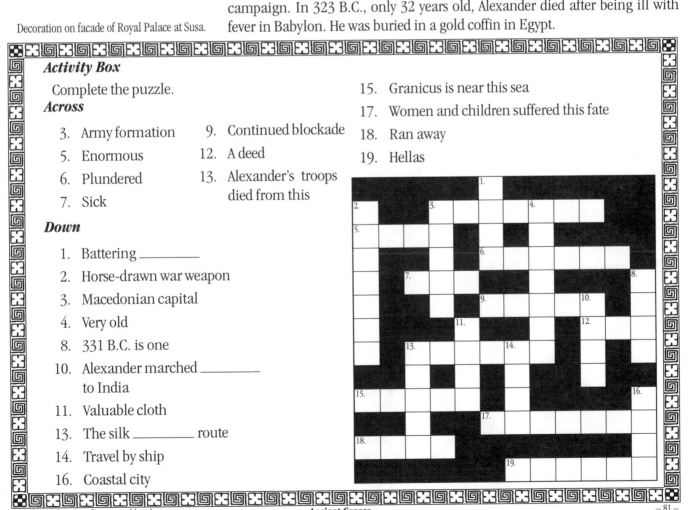

Activity Box

Complete the puzzle.

Across

3. Army formation
5. Enormous
6. Plundered
7. Sick
9. Continued blockade
12. A deed
13. Alexander's troops died from this
15. Granicus is near this sea
17. Women and children suffered this fate
18. Ran away
19. Hellas

Down

1. Battering _____
2. Horse-drawn war weapon
3. Macedonian capital
4. Very old
8. 331 B.C. is one
10. Alexander marched _____ to India
11. Valuable cloth
13. The silk _____ route
14. Travel by ship
16. Coastal city

THE ROMAN THREAT

Teacher's Notes

Philip V also had plans to extend his kingdom to territories closer to Rome along the Adriatic Sea.

The Greeks at Cynoscephalae used the phalanx, but Roman battle tactics using elephants and changing attack plans helped to defeat Philip's army. Both armies had about 25,000 men and the Roman forces were commanded by Quinctius Flamininus.

The Seleucid Empire was the eastern part of Alexander the Great's empire and was ruled by descendants of Seleucus, one of Alexander's generals.

Paulus had never fought against a Greece phalanx, but observed gaps in the battle formation as it moved across uneven ground. Perseus was later captured and incarcerated in a Roman prison where he died. The battle of Pydna ended the kingdom of Macedonia, which Rome divided into four republics.

A rebellion in Corinth in 146 B.C. was severely dealt with, the city was utterly destroyed and its citizens killed or forced into slavery.

Ancient Greece

THE ROMAN THREAT

After Rome had defeated its main rival, Carthage, and its general, Hannibal, the Romans decided to take action against Philip V of Macedonia in 200 B.C., for the Greek king had made a peace treaty with Hannibal. A three-year war ended with the battle of Cynoscephalae. The Romans lost around 700 soldiers but 8,000 Greek soldiers lost their lives and thousands were taken prisoner. Philip left the battlefield when he realized he had lost.

When the Romans left Greece in 194 B.C., Antiochus III, king of Syria and the Seleucid Empire, decided to attack Greece, but his army of over 70,000 men was defeated at Magnesia in 190 B.C. by the Roman army of only 30,000 under the command of Lucius Scipio. Rome then made Antiochus sign a treaty forcing him to leave Asia Minor with his army.

In later years, Perseus, son of Philip V, wanted Macedonia to become independent of Roman rule, but in 168 B.C. Rome sent a strong army under a general called Lucius Paulus. In 167 B.C. at Pydna, his troops drove through gaps in the Greek phalanx and the Greeks were defeated. Perseus fled and over 20,000 Greeks were slain, while thousands more became slaves.

Over 20 years after the battle of Pydna, rebellions in Macedonia, Corinth and some other city-states were harshly dealt with and many Greek lives were lost. From then on most of Alexander's old empire fell into Roman hands.

Activity Box

1. What year was the battle of Cynoscephalae?

   _____

2. Roman soldiers are called

   _____.

3. Why did Rome fight against Philip V?

   _____

   _____

4. Who ruled the Seleucid Empire?

   _____

5. Which battle did Lucius Paulus win?

   _____

6. What happened to the prisoners of war?

   _____

7. Which general was Rome's chief rival?

   _____

8. How many years were there between the battles of Pydna and Magnesia?

   _____

9. Whose army defeated a military force more than twice the size of his army?

   _____

10. Cynoscephalae lies (NW, south, SW) of Pydna.

    _____

TECHNOLOGY

Teacher's Notes

Archimedes was born in Syracuse, a Greek colony, around 287 B.C. He produced original work in astronomy, engineering and mathematics, and was the first to calculate the value of pi(π), which is the symbol representing the relationship between the diameter and circumference of a circle. He was aware of how levers and pulleys worked and designed machines which could raise heavy weights with little human effort. He was killed by a Roman soldier when Syracuse fell to Roman forces in 212 B.C.

Hero lived in the Greek city of Alexandria around 30 A.D. We know from his written records that he invented a wine dispenser worked by a coin in a slot. His screw press for grapes or olives was used for centuries before it was superseded.

No paintings or sketches of Greek cranes from the Classical Age (500–300 B.C.) have been found, though Aristotle's descriptions tell us that rather complicated pulley systems and windlasses were in use in the fourth century B.C. Archimedes is believed to have invented the multiple pulley.

TECHNOLOGY

Apart from their development of war weapons, the Greeks made technological advances in other areas too. Complete the passages with the given words to discover some details about these examples of Greek technology.

1.

end	handle	brilliant	century	river	Greece	turned	mounted
used	higher	evidence	water	pump	invented	section	

The most _____[1] scientist in ancient _____[2]

was Archimedes. Though firm _____[3] is lacking, the

Archimedean _____[4] for raising water to _____[5]

levels was probably _____[6] by him. The pump could be _____[7] on wooden posts on

a _____[8] bank with one _____[9] in the _____[10]. As the pump was

_____[11] with the feet or a simple _____[12], water was lifted along each

_____[13]. It was still being _____[14] in the 20th _____[15].

Archimedes Screw

2.

sphere	spouts	lawn	heated	provide	invention	poured	toy
scientist	engine	boiler	friends	principle	mounted	forerunner	

Hero's Aeoliphile

Hero was a _____[1] whose most ingenious _____[2] was the

"aeoliphile," a _____[3] of the steam _____[4]. It was a hollow

_____[5] with two hooked spouts and was _____[6] above a

_____[7] containing water. The water was _____[8] and the

steam which _____[9] from the _____[10] rotated the sphere.

The same _____[11] is used in _____[12] sprinklers and jet

engines. Hero's invention was a _____[13] to amuse _____[14]

and was never developed to _____[15] steam power.

3.

engineer	marble	heavy	ropes	blocks	braced	position	windlass
sideways	crane	base	used	lengths	spread	temples	

This type of Greek _____[1] using pulleys and a _____[2] was described by a

Roman _____[3]. Two large _____[4] of timber were _____[5]

at the top, _____[6] at the base and held up by _____[7].

Cranes would have been _____[8] to raise the _____[9]

blocks of stone or _____[10] in the construction of _____[11]

and public buildings. Some _____[12] movement in the

_____[13] meant that the large _____[14]

could be maneuvred into _____[15].

Greek Crane

pulleys

windlass

ENTERTAINMENT–SYMPOSIA

Teacher's Notes

A "symposiarchos" ("master of drinking") would be chosen to select the proportion of wine to water, regulate the supply of alcohol and oversee the number of cups drunk by each guest. The drink was usually two or three parts water to one part wine, less alcohol content than modern beer. Though many symposia were serious discussions, some guests became drunk and there are accounts of vandalism as they staggered home.

Guests who were too drunk to walk would be taken home by slaves. Finding slaves to serve at symposia was not a problem as there were thousands of slaves in Greece over the centuries. The total in Athens over the years has been estimated at between 60,000 and 80,000.

The Greek philosopher Plato (in an account called "Symposium"), and the soldier historian Xenophon, both recorded events which took place at a drinking party attended by Plato.

Discussion for some guests would often last through the night and some of the best poetry of Ancient Greece was written to entertain guests at these important social gatherings.

There may have been similar parties for females but no recorded evidence to support this theory has been found.

ENTERTAINMENT—SYMPOSIA

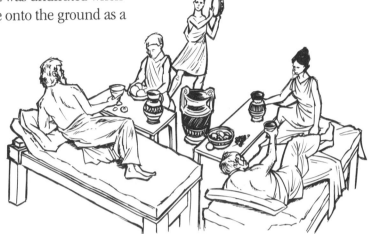

The Greek "symposium" (a drinking party) was at the center of any ancient Greek city's political, social and cultural life. It was particularly popular in the homes of wealthy, aristocratic Athenians. Scenes from these symposia are often shown in paintings on ancient Greek drinking cups and vases. The guests, men only, would lounge on couches in the villa's men's room ("andron") and be served food and wine by slaves, while musicians, often flute girls, and dancers would entertain them. The dancers were girls or young, handsome boys. Wine was usually mixed with water as Greeks thought it was dangerous and barbaric to drink pure wine, but it was undiluted when guests offered a libation (a ritual of pouring wine onto the ground as a sacrifice to a god) to Dionysus, the god of wine.

Later in the evening the guests would turn to the main purpose of the evening—discussion on a variety of topics such as the meaning of life, the nature of love and friendship, or the political or military problems of the times. The discussion was often led by famous guests like the philosopher, Socrates, or Aristophanes, a famous writer of comic plays.

Activity Box

Color in this scene from a symposium.

What do you think of the Greek custom of preventing women from attending a symposium, even one held in their own home?

_____

_____

_____

_____

ENTERTAINMENT–THEATER

Teacher's Notes

The first actor to interact in dialogues with the chorus was a poet called Thespis, hence our word "thespian" for an actor.

Aristophanes, a great writer of comedies, won first prize for several plays—"Babylonians," "Archanians" and "Knights." His comedy, "Clouds," was about new ways of learning in education and a strong city-state which dominated others. It was an attack on Athens and only won third prize.

Two "obols" were equivalent to a day's wage for the average worker.

Until the 20th century, the only Greek plays in existence were tragedies by Aeschylus, Sophocles and Euripides and comedies by Aristophanes. Then, in 1959, a comedy by another Greek writer was published after it was found in Egypt. Tragedies were generally about conflict between gods and humans. A day's program at a festival would have three tragedies followed by a comedy. There were no censorship laws such as we have today and many comedies were extremely rude.

Women appear to have been in the audiences during the fourth century B.C., but experts are not certain they were allowed to attend in the fifth century B.C.

The huge, covered theater in Athens had a wooden roof made from the timber of captured Persian ships and almost 100 columns. It was built by Pericles and called the "odeion" (the name "Odeon" was given to many 20th century cinemas).

All the great dramatists of the fifth century B.C. were Athenians, but by the following century they had passed into history. The play "Medea" (an enchantress in Greek myths) was written by Euripides and is still performed in theaters today.

Additional Activity

Follow this procedure to make your own actor's mask.

1. Cut out the shape of your mask from card stock. Make eye/mouth holes.

2. Build up your mask with papier-mâché. Make sure cheeks, eyebrows, chin and lips are built up so they can be seen from a distance.

3. If you are going to use a stick to hold your mask (as shown), fix it in place on the back.

4. While it is drying, curve the mask so it will fit around your face (use an rubber band or string).

5. Paint your mask with vivid colors and when it is dry give it two coats of varnish.

Stick for actor to hold mask

Ancient Greece

ENTERTAINMENT-THEATER

The ancient Greeks founded the theater we know today. Their dramas began as rituals at several annual religious festivals for their gods, held at different times of the year. Choral songs were recited or sung and in the sixth century B.C., dialogues between one actor and the chorus were introduced. The following century brought plays which competed for an ivory crown awarded to the best comedy and tragedy. Eventually there were three types of plays—tragedies about serious matters, comedies to make people laugh, and satires to ridicule flaws in individuals and society. They were usually told in verse. People came from all over the Greek world to watch them and scenes from these popular plays are painted on many ancient Greek vases

Masks worn by actors

Both faces of a theater entry token found in Athens

Audiences were always ready to hiss or boo the actors, even throwing stones, nuts, or fruit on occasions. Tragedies were generally about Greek heroes or heroines and, though audiences knew the stories, they liked to see how the dramatists told the tales in different ways. The program lasted all day from dawn, with audiences watching several plays and eating food during the intervals between performances. It cost two metal discs ("obols") to get in but the poorest families were paid for by the city-state.

All actors were men; they also played the female roles. They wore appropriate masks for the parts they played and female masks were usually painted white. The masks were enlarged so the audience could see them from a distance in the large theater. They could be made of strips of linen pasted together, wood or even metal.

Every large Greek city had a huge, open-air theater, often built into the side of a hill for easier construction. The stepped seats looked down on the stage, which wasn't raised in the early theaters. Important citizens like judges, priests, or political leaders had the best seats. There was a permanent wooden or stone structure (a "skene") at the rear of the stage where actors changed costumes before entering the stage through a central door. There were no curtains as we have in today's theaters.

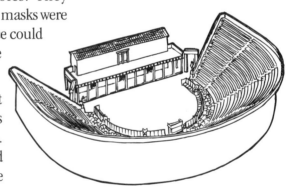

The open-air theater at Epidauros is still used every summer to show ancient Greek plays to residents and tourists.

Activity Box

Name the three types of plays.

_____ _____ _____

2. List a fact on each of the following topics to do with Greek theater.

men: _____

masks: _____

food: _____

stage: _____

judges: _____

ENTERTAINMENT–CHILDREN'S GAMES

Teacher's Notes

Pottery dolls and wooden chariots were some of the toys made by those slaves who were skilled craftsmen. Dolls of cloth and wood were probably popular too, but do not survive the hundreds of years since they were made.

In the afternoons, boys went to training grounds ("palaistra") for physical education, which included ball games and tag.

Experts believe the Greeks almost certainly played soccer. The Romans admired the Greeks and copied many of their customs, and soccer was popular on the streets of Ancient Rome.

Another Greek vase shows boys playing a ball game with one player sitting on the shoulders of another. This game was popular and was also played by girls, but experts are not sure about the rules. It was still being played in northern Greece in the 19th century but the more modern rules may have been different.

Additional Activity

An ancient Greek games session could be arranged where students rotate around a series of games played by the children of that era. Rules could be discussed beforehand and a set of rules designed for each station.

ENTERTAINMENT–CHILDREN'S GAMES

Pig rattle

Many toys, not much different in appearance from modern playthings, have been found in excavations, especially rattles and balls. Archaeologists have also found dolls, tops, hoops and kites. The dolls were usually made from fired clay and some had jointed arms and legs.

Jointed doll found in Athens

Children played blindman's bluff, tug-of-war and skittles. They played marbles with walnuts and knucklebones with small pieces of bone from sheep. They also played leapfrog, and ancient Greek pottery shows children bowling hoops.

Team games were also played but little is known about the rules. This Greek vase (below) shows boys playing a game like cricket. One boy is throwing a ball while another is ready to catch it if it misses what appears to be a wicket. This game has been called "ephedrismos" but the rules are not known. Part of a marble relief sculpture (below) in an Athens museum shows boys playing a game very similar to hockey. All children played games in the nude in Sparta, a custom other Greek city states deplored.

A game resembling hockey

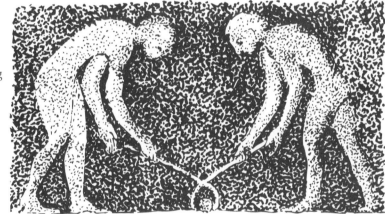

Greek vase shows boys playing a game like cricket.

Activity Box

Follow the procedure and make your own knucklebones.

1. Cut/tear newspaper into small pieces.

2. Mix equal amounts of paste and water.

3. Stir the paper and paste together to make papier-mâché.

4. Mold the paper into knucklebone shapes as shown.

5. Let them dry, then paint them a bone color.

6. Play the ancient Greek game with a partner by throwing the "bones" into the air and catching them on the back of your hand.

Note: We don't know much about ancient Greek rules; so make up your own.

Model of girls playing knucklebones

Knucklebones found in the agora in Athens

GREAT MEN OF THE CLASSICAL AGE
(500–300 B.C.)

Teacher's Notes

Socrates:

Socrates walked the streets of Athens barefoot and wearing dirty robes, but he changed the thinking of his contemporaries with ideas which questioned the validity of gods and led Greeks to more scientific thought. Ancient Greek ideas still shape our world today.

Socrates was charged with "not recognizing the gods that the city recognizes." His defense speeches and those of his accuser, a religious fanatic called Meletus, were timed by a water clock as each speaker had a fixed time.

Hemlock causes very painful paralysis of the nervous system.

Aristotle: Aristotle's interest covered all fields of knowledge from astronomy to politics and logic to literature. His account of the male octopus using a specially developed tentacle during mating was confirmed in 1842. His description of the unusual breeding habits of a Greek catfish was supported in 1856. Most of the important writings of Aristotle have survived.

Pericles: Pericles' building program, apart from the beautiful Parthenon temple to the goddess Athena and other impressive buildings, also included defensive walls, harbors and storehouses to promote trade. He used money left over from building to pay for ships for the powerful Athenian navy.

Pericles was made leader of Athens in 460 B.C. and presided over a period known as the "Golden Age," during which he encouraged Greek art and drama.

He persuaded Athens to fight Sparta because "from the greatest dangers comes the greatest glory."

GREAT MEN OF THE CLASSICAL AGE (500–300 B.C.)

Use the given words to compete the information on great Greeks.

1. Socrates (ca. 469–399 B.C.)

writings	tried	influencing	thinkers	drinking
evidence	exile	questioning	students	power

Socrates was the first of the great _____[1] of Athens. We see his ideas in

the _____[2] of historian Xenophon, and the _____[3] of

Socrates, especially the great philosopher, Plato, for there is no _____[4]

Socrates recorded anything in writing. For _____[5] the Athenian dreams of _____[6]

and the way his society functioned (thus _____[7] his young followers), Socrates was

_____[8] and given the choice of _____[9] or death. He chose to die by

_____[10] hemlock, a deadly poison.

2. Aristotle (384–322 B.C.)

ridiculed	zoologists	biology	spread	tutor
reference	influential	learning	student	plants

Aristotle, one of Ancient Greece's most _____[1] thinkers, founded the

science of _____[2]. Without microscopes or _____[3]

books, he studied and classified _____[4] and over 500 animal types.

Several discoveries were _____[5] for centuries until proven to be correct

by _____[6] in the 19th century. In 342 B.C. he became _____[7]

to Alexander the Great, who later _____[8] Aristotle's ideas throughout the Greek world. Aristotle, a

_____[9] of Plato, eventually set up his own _____[10] center, the Lyceum, in Athens.

3. Pericles (ca. 490–429 B.C.)

plague	Athens	leader	public	Persians
Sparta	elected	power	ordinary	organized

A great political _____[1] of Athens, Pericles was also a popularly

_____[2] Athenian general who fought against the _____[3]

and other Greek city-states. He stripped the aristocrats of their _____[4]

and made government positions more available to _____[5] Athenians.

He wanted to make _____[6] a great and attractive city so he _____[7] the

construction of beautiful temples and _____[8] buildings. He died from the _____[9]

during a siege of Athens by rival city-state _____[10].

IN THE NEWS!

Teacher's Notes

The comedy "Lysistrata" was written in 411 B.C. by Aristophanes, who proposed a plot where wives would not live with their husbands until they made peace. It was his only women's play and one of the few ancient comedies which appeals to modern audiences.

The original Colossus of Rhodes was thought to be 30 meters tall and made from the melted weapons of defeated invaders. It was started in 290 B.C., took 12 years to build and, according to ancient books, was made of bronze. It was dedicated to the sun god Helios. The Rhodes council approved over $45 million for the project to build a new one.

Former Australian Prime Ministers Gough Whitlam and Malcolm Fraser have tried to persuade Britain to hand back the Elgin Marbles. There are 56 blocks of statues from the Parthenon being held in London; 40 more are in Athens. In today's heavily polluted Athens, no one expects the statues will be put back on the temple if they are returned.

The Pharos stood about 135 meters high and was badly damaged by an earthquake after standing for centuries. The city of Alexandria has practically nothing that can be seen from its glorious past.

In July 2000, the Australian government returned a hoard of stolen artifacts to Greece. The hoard was traced to a Greek-Australian man and included urns, jugs and bowls up to 2,800 years old and worth at least $4 million.

A Greek farmer recently stumbled across a rare, solid gold wreath which was found to be 2,250 years old. Only the third of its kind found in Greece, it weighed over half a kilogram. According to Greek law, people who find artifacts and report their discovery to the appropriate authority are entitled to a percentage of the object's value.

IN THE NEWS!

"Neglected Wives"

The Year 12 Dance and Drama students of Ocean Reef Senior High School in Perth, Western Australia, recently performed an adapted version of "Lysistrata," an ancient Greek comedy. It describes how the wives in those times felt neglected by their husbands who were away fighting on the battlefields.

"A Colossal Task!"

A local council on the Greek island of Rhodes has plans to rebuild the Colossus of Rhodes, one of the seven wonders of the ancient world. The original giant statue was destroyed by an earthquake. Arabs who occupied Rhodes centuries after it was built sold the remains for scrap metal. The council had hoped that the replica would be completed and be a tourist attraction for the 2004 Olympic Games in Athens.

"Historic Find"

The Pharos, one of the seven wonders of the ancient world, was a gigantic lighthouse built in the Greek city of Alexandria, which was founded by Alexander the Great. After its destruction by an earthquake, the rubble lay under the sea for centuries. In 1995, parts of the building were raised from the seabed.

"Trireme Trial"

A modern full-sized trireme, an ancient Mediterranean warship, was built, launched and tested on the Aegean Sea near Greece in 1987. The trial proved that the large Greek warships must have been driven by three banks of oars with a man on each, rather than three men to each oar.

"Marbles"

Important people around the world have been trying to persuade Britain to return the Elgin Marbles to Greece. The sculptured marble statues, created in the fifth century B.C., were part of a frieze decorating the Parthenon, a beautiful temple built for the goddess Athena in Athens. After observing the deterioration of many of the statues, Lord Elgin used his influence as British ambassador to remove them and sell them to the British Museum.

Activity Box

1. Which word means "a copy of a work of art"?

   _____

2. What kind of play is "Lysistrata"?

   _____

3. Do you think the Elgin Marbles should be returned to Greece? _____

   Why? _____

   _____

4. What is a frieze?

   _____

5. Why did the Rhodes council plan to build a new Colossus of Rhodes?

   _____

6. Where was the trireme model tested?

   _____

7. Who took the marble statues from Athens?

   _____

8. Which word from the news items means "ignored"?

   _____

9. Who invaded the island of Rhodes?

   _____

10. What kind of building was the Pharos?

    _____

THEIR LEGACY

Teacher's Notes

The term "classical architecture" refers to the building styles developed by the ancient Greeks and Romans, though the origin of these styles can be traced back to the Minoans and Mycenaeans.

Doric columns were named after the Dorians, Ionic after the region of Ionia and Corinthian after the city-state of Corinth. Doric columns were the least decorative, Ionic had spiral scrolls at the corners and the Corinthian, the most slender style, were decorated with acanthus leaves at the top (the capital). Doric columns were used between 700 B.C. and 600 B.C., Ionic from around 500 B.C., and Corinthian from 400 B.C. onwards.

Part of the Parthenon was constructed using the "golden rectangle," whose proportions of length to width were in the ratio of approximately 1.6 to 1. Such rectangles are still said to be more pleasing to the eye than other rectangles, but no one can say why! The great 20th century French architect Corbusier obviously thought so, because he used the golden rectangle in some of his designs.

Additional activity

1. Draw your own golden rectangles by selecting various widths then multiplying each width by 1.6 (calculator) to complete the rectangle.

2. Draw rectangles without measurements shown. Trade with a partner. Then work out which ones are golden rectangles by measuring the width and multiplying it by 1.6 to see if the length is correct, or dividing the length by the width and the answer should be 1.6.

Nearly all European art has been strongly influenced by the creative work done by the ancient Greeks.

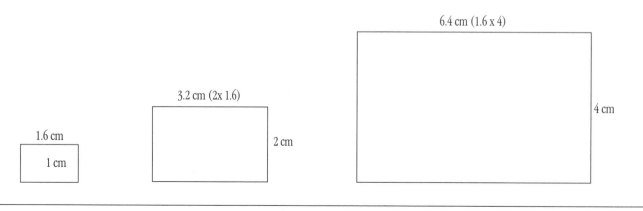

Ancient Greece

THEIR LEGACY

There are many democracies in the world today, but the idea of ordinary citizens having a say, through some kind of voting system, in how their country functions, stems from the ancient Greek world.

The Greek language, the origin of so many English words, helped to spread Christianity, for the Gospels in the Bible were written in Greek, and today there are millions of Christians in all parts of the globe.

Classical Greek architecture has been copied in many buildings in cities around the world. The most famous ancient Greek contribution to architecture was a set of styles for columns used in temples. The three main columns are Doric, Ionic and Corinthian. The British Museum in London has Ionic columns and decorative reliefs like those in ancient Greece. Many existing 18th and 19th century houses in the world's great cities have a temple triangle over the main door and Doric columns on either side.

Doric style Ionic style Corinthian style

When you enjoy a performance at the theater today, remember that many modern theaters follow ancient Greek designs and the world of theater was one of the greatest contributions to world culture by the city of Athens.

Apart from some wonderful buildings still standing and craftwork of the highest order displayed in the world's museums, the ancient Greeks have left behind what could be called an "empire of the mind," for theories and teachings by the great Greek scholars are still discussed in schools and institutions today.

Activity Box

List examples of ancient Greek legacy in your life or area.

_____ _____

_____ _____

_____ _____

_____ _____

LEGENDS (1)

Greek legends were handed down orally from generation to generation by storytellers who crisscrossed the ancient Greek world telling the stories of Greek heroes and heroines. They were eventually inscribed on clay tablets and then on paper made from papyrus plants. They are still read today after thousands of years.

Jason and the Golden Fleece

1. Use the given words to complete this Greek legend.

ship	plotting	Fleece	fogs	claims	dragon	sail	murdered	throne	discover
seas	driven	palace	falls	obtain	brother	leaves	guarded	return	smuggled

Jason's father is _____[1] from his throne in Iolcos by his own _____[2], the tyrant Pelias, so Jason is _____[3] away and raised by the centaur Chiron. Years later, Jason _____[4] his right to rule, but Pelias promises the _____[5] only if Jason brings back the Golden _____[6], which is fastened to an oak tree and _____[7] by a dragon which never sleeps. On his _____[8], the "Argo," Jason and his Argonauts _____[9] across the Aegean and Mediterranean _____[10], through storms and dense _____[11]. When they reach the _____[12] at Colchis the king's daughter, Medea, _____[13] in love with Jason and wants to _____[14] to Greece as his wife. She helps him to _____ the Golden Fleece by giving the _____[16] a sleeping potion, but warns Jason that her father is _____[17] to kill him. They escape with the fleece but _____[18] that Jason's father has been _____[19] by Pelias. They eventually settle in Corinth until Jason _____[20] Medea for the daughter of the Corinthian king.

Jason

2. Now the legend is complete, answer the following questions.

(a) What name is given to the crew of the "Argo"?

_____

(b) Give words from the passage which mean

(i) thick _____

(ii) conspiring _____

(c) Why do you think Jason was smuggled away?

_____

_____

(d) Why did Medea help Jason?

_____

(e) How did she help him? _____

_____

(f) Why was the voyage to Colchis difficult?

_____

_____

(g) Who are the two villains in the story?

_____

(h) Jason remains with Medea for the rest of his life. True or false?

_____

(i) Use your dictionary and explain what a tyrant is.

_____

_____

Ancient Greece

LEGENDS (2)

The story of the legendary city of Troy is described in Homer's "Iliad." It was believed to be a mythical place. However, a German businessman called Heinrich Schliemann, who had read Greek legends as a boy, believed there was such a city and that it could be found in modern Turkey. In the 1870s his workers removed tons of soil from a hill called Hissarlik and came across the remains of a city that had been rebuilt several times over the centuries. They unearthed golden ornaments which Schliemann called "King Priam's Treasure." Experts now believe it is the site of Troy, a city which may have attracted the Greeks, not because they wanted to rescue the legendary Helen, but because its position enabled it to control trade through the Hellespont (the modern Dardanelles).

A wooden model of the Trojan horse in modern Troy. Ladders enable children to climb inside like the Greek soldiers.

The Wooden Horse of Troy

Complete the legend by using the given words.

rest	heroes	Achilles	hiding	thousand	kidnapped	pretended
gift	ruled	defended	fought	besieged	celebrated	ruler
gates	horse	warriors	husband	returned	success	

Many years ago, Greek soldiers _____[1] a 10-year war against King Priam, _____[2] of the walled city of Troy. Priam's son, Paris, had _____[3] Helen, the beautiful young wife of Menelaus, who _____[4] Sparta. The Greek army of 50,000 men was led by Odysseus, _____[5] and Ajax, who were famous _____[6] of Greek legend. The fleet of a _____[7] ships sailed for Troy and _____[8] the city, which was _____[9] by Hector, the greatest of Trojan _____[10].

After years of fighting without _____[11], the Greeks built a huge wooden _____[12] which they left outside Troy's walls as a _____[13]. The Greek fleet then _____[14] to sail away, so the Trojans _____[15] and hauled the horse into the city. Greek soldiers were _____[16] inside the horse and at night they opened the city _____[17] to let in the Greek army from the ships which had secretly _____[18]. Helen went back to her _____[19] and lived in peace for the _____[20] of her life.

ERATOSTHENES

Eratosthenes was a brilliant ancient Greek mathematician. He was born in the third century B.C. in Cyrene, a Greek town in North Africa. His knowledge covered a wide range of topics few scholars have managed to achieve. He wrote expertly on geography, astronomy, chronology and mathematics, and devised a calendar which included leap years.

Perhaps his greatest achievement was working out the circumference of the Earth by measuring the length of shadows cast by the sun in different places. He did this without leaving North Africa and his calculations revealed an error of only 3 $\frac{1}{2}$%.

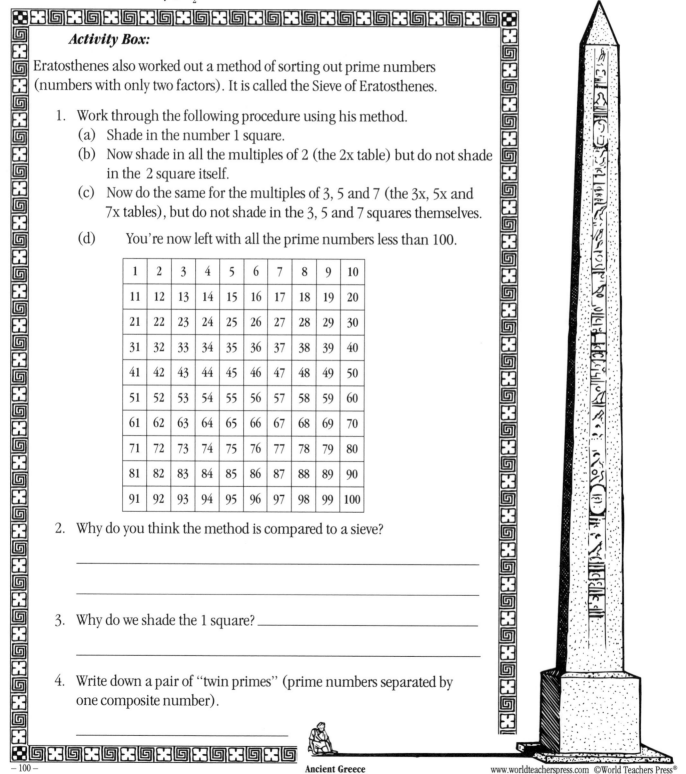

Activity Box:

Eratosthenes also worked out a method of sorting out prime numbers (numbers with only two factors). It is called the Sieve of Eratosthenes.

1. Work through the following procedure using his method.
    (a) Shade in the number 1 square.
    (b) Now shade in all the multiples of 2 (the 2x table) but do not shade in the 2 square itself.
    (c) Now do the same for the multiples of 3, 5 and 7 (the 3x, 5x and 7x tables), but do not shade in the 3, 5 and 7 squares themselves.

    (d)   You're now left with all the prime numbers less than 100.

1	2	3	4	5	6	7	8	9	10
11	12	13	14	15	16	17	18	19	20
21	22	23	24	25	26	27	28	29	30
31	32	33	34	35	36	37	38	39	40
41	42	43	44	45	46	47	48	49	50
51	52	53	54	55	56	57	58	59	60
61	62	63	64	65	66	67	68	69	70
71	72	73	74	75	76	77	78	79	80
81	82	83	84	85	86	87	88	89	90
91	92	93	94	95	96	97	98	99	100

2. Why do you think the method is compared to a sieve?

    _____

    _____

3. Why do we shade the 1 square? _____

    _____

4. Write down a pair of "twin primes" (prime numbers separated by one composite number).

    _____

Ancient Greece

LANGUAGE (1)

You can open up at random any page in a large English dictionary and somewhere on that page there will almost certainly be a word derived from the Greek language. See if you find out the English words derived from the ancient Greek words listed. Spelling must be correct! Write each word in a sentence to show its meaning.

	Greek word	Meaning of Greek word	English word	Meaning of English word
1.	polis	A town	metro __ __ __ __ __	A large town or city
2.	demos	the people	demo __ __ __ __ __	rule by the people
3.	athlein	to compete	ath __ __ __ __	a sports competitor
4.	skene	permanent stage background	sc __ __ __	setting for a play
5.	Draco	an Athenian lawmaker	draco __ __ __ __	harsh, strict
6.	thronos	seat of honor in a house	th __ __ __ __	royal seat
7.	idiotai	amateurs or ignorant people	id __ __ __ __	fools
8.	ankyra	a hook	an __ __ __ __	ship's device
9.	Olympia	site of ancient Games	Oly __ __ __ __	period of time between Olympic Games
10.	biblion	book	B __ __ __ __	holy book
11.	mikros	small	micro __ __ __ __ __ __	very small
12.	domos	a house	dom __ __ __ __	relating to a home

LANGUAGE

	Greek word	Meaning of Greek word	English word	Meaning of English word
13.	Atlas	mythical giant holding the world on his shoulders	a _ _ _ _	book of maps
14.	Hector	boastful Trojan hero	hec _ _ _	to bully
15.	Laconia	Greek region where people said very little	lac _ _ _ _	brief in speech
16.	Stentor	loud-voiced Greek herald in Homer's "Iliad"	stent _ _ _ _ _	very loud
17.	kritai	judges	cri _ _ _ _	people who judge
18.	Tantalus	mythical Greek king	tant _ _ _ _ _	to tease
19.	Thespis	Greek poet/actor	thes _ _ _ _	an actor or actress
20.	Hades	Greek god – ruler of the underworld	H _ _ _ _	hell
21	stadion	fixed length of a race	sta _ _ _ _	sports arena
22.	athlon	a contest	dec _ _ _ _ _ _	contest with ten events
23.	planetes	a wanderer	pl _ _ _ _	heavenly body
24.	Hypokrites	an actor	hyp _ _ _ _ _ _	one who pretends to be what he isn't
25.	xenoi	foreigners	xeno _ _ _ _ _	fear of foreigners

SEVEN WONDERS OF THE ANCIENT WORLD

The "Seven Wonders of the Ancient World" were first listed by the Greeks in the third century B.C. and mentioned in a poem by Greek poet, Antipater, about 100 years later. Only the Egyptian pyramids can be seen today. Seven was a mystical number made up of two lucky numbers, 4 and 3 (e.g., 7 planets, 7 deadly sins, Shakespeare's "Seven Ages of Man"). The five wonders shown all have a Greek connection: the Mausoleum at Halicarnassus was designed by Greek architect, Pythius, and another Greek architect, Sostratos, built the Pharos. Ephesus, Rhodes and Olympia were all places in the Greek world.

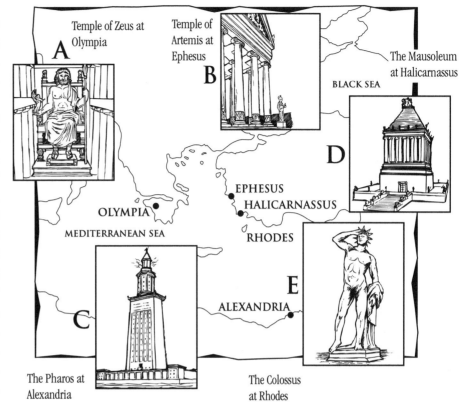

Temple of Zeus at Olympia — A

Temple of Artemis at Ephesus — B

The Mausoleum at Halicarnassus — D

BLACK SEA

EPHESUS
HALICARNASSUS

RHODES

OLYMPIA

MEDITERRANEAN SEA

The Pharos at Alexandria — C

ALEXANDRIA

The Colossus at Rhodes — E

Activity Box

1. Use reference sources and write your own sentence about each wonder above.

   (a) _____

   _____

   (b) _____

   _____

   (c) _____

   _____

   (d) _____

   _____

   (e) _____

   _____

2. Which of the "Seven Wonders of the Ancient World" is not mentioned on this worksheet?

   _____

REVIEW QUIZ (1)

Use your memory and your notes to check the correct answer.

1. Military Formation
   (a) Minoan ☐
   (b) Iliad ☐
   (c) Phalanx ☐

2. Greek Letter
   (a) Zota ☐
   (b) Alpha ☐
   (c) Ata ☐

3. Military State
   (a) Sparta ☐
   (b) Corinth ☐
   (c) Iona ☐

4. Water Plant
   (a) Omega ☐
   (b) Papyrus ☐
   (c) Dorian ☐

5. Area around Athens
   (a) Laconia ☐
   (b) Attica ☐
   (c) Athenian ☐

6. Magistrate
   (a) Archon ☐
   (b) Delta ☐
   (c) Tyrant ☐

7. Marketplace
   (a) Oracle ☐
   (b) Agora ☐
   (c) Hades ☐

8. A Chair
   (a) Andron ☐
   (b) Omega ☐
   (c) Thronos ☐

9. Trading goods for other goods
   (a) Charter ☐
   (b) Zeta ☐
   (c) Barter ☐

10. Foreign Residents
    (a) Helots ☐
    (b) Metics ☐
    (c) Archons ☐

11. Teacher
    (a) Grammatist ☐
    (b) Agora ☐
    (c) Delta ☐

12. Writing Tool
    (a) Omega ☐
    (b) Abacus ☐
    (c) Stylus ☐

13. A Tunic
    (a) Upsilon ☐
    (b) Chiton ☐
    (c) Spartan ☐

14. Male Party
    (a) Amber ☐
    (b) Oracle ☐
    (c) Symposium ☐

15. Tile Picture/Design
    (a) Beta ☐
    (b) Mosaic ☐
    (c) Tempera ☐

16. Period of Time
    (a) Oracle ☐
    (b) Zeus ☐
    (c) Olympiad ☐

17. Spartan Slaves
    (a) Archons ☐
    (b) Aristocrats ☐
    (c) Helots ☐

18. Pottery Jar
    (a) Amphora ☐
    (b) Cyrene ☐
    (c) Archom ☐

19. "Father of Medicine"
    (a) Pericles ☐
    (b) Hippocrates ☐
    (c) Achilles ☐

20. Theater Entry Token
    (a) Obol ☐
    (b) Eta ☐
    (c) Cyrene ☐

Ancient Greece

REVIEW QUIZ (2)

21. Olympic Event

    (a) Rotation ☐
    (b) Demeter ☐
    (c) Pankration ☐

22. Leader of Gods

    (a) Hera ☐
    (b) Zeus ☐
    (c) Pericles ☐

23. Body Scraper

    (a) Strigil ☐
    (b) Stylus ☐
    (c) Hellus ☐

24. Goddess

    (a) Homer ☐
    (b) Pheidias ☐
    (c) Athena ☐

25. Leg Armor
    (a) Hopla ☐
    (b) Greaves ☐
    (c) Cuirass ☐

26. Body Armor
    (a) Hopla ☐
    (b) Greaves ☐
    (c) Cuirass ☐

27. Shield
    (a) Greave ☐
    (b) Hopla ☐
    (c) Cuirass ☐

28. Greek Warship
    (a) Upsilon ☐
    (b) Andron ☐
    (c) Trireme ☐

29. Persian King
    (a) Miletus ☐
    (b) Darius ☐
    (c) Hera ☐

30. Son of Philip II
    (a) Pericles ☐
    (b) Themistocles ☐
    (c) Alexander ☐

31. Alexander's Horse
    (a) Upsilon ☐
    (b) Bucephalus ☐
    (c) Xerxes ☐

32. Persian Capital
    (a) Pella ☐
    (b) Tyre ☐
    (c) Persepolis ☐

33. Men's Room

    (a) Archon ☐
    (b) Andron ☐
    (c) Libation ☐

34. Serious Play

    (a) Tragedy ☐
    (b) Skene ☐
    (c) Agora ☐

35. Used to Make Bronze

    (a) Lead ☐
    (b) Iron ☐
    (c) Copper ☐

36. Greek Poet

    (a) Darius ☐
    (b) Homer ☐
    (c) Ares ☐

37. Ruling Group

    (a) Domos ☐
    (b) Oligarchy ☐
    (c) Sigma ☐

38. Foot Soldier

    (a) Hoplite ☐
    (b) Hopla ☐
    (c) Obol ☐

39. Hoisting Machine

    (a) Hoplite ☐
    (b) Windlass ☐
    (c) Gamma ☐

40. Year of first Ancient Olympics
    (a) ca. 400 B.C. ☐
    (b) ca. 254 B.C. ☐
    (c) ca. 776 B.C. ☐

REVIEW WORD SEARCH

Find the answers in the word search and slot them into the correct clue. This should be your final activity when all worksheets are completed.

B	G	T	H	E	B	E	S	X	M	L	P	O	E	M	S
R	R	A	T	T	L	E	S	W	A	T	H	E	N	S	O
O	A	N	T	O	R	T	O	I	S	E	I	B	X	T	M
N	I	S	A	L	A	M	I	S	K	P	L	A	G	U	E
Z	N	I	P	I	R	A	T	E	S	E	I	T	E	W	G
E	Z	E	U	S	C	S	E	B	J	R	P	T	O	H	A
X	T	G	O	E	H	E	L	L	A	S	B	I	P	E	L
O	R	E	L	L	I	N	S	O	S	E	L	C	E	R	Y
A	I	L	Y	E	M	S	P	O	O	P	H	A	R	O	S
R	R	I	M	P	E	F	A	M	N	O	T	W	I	D	A
M	E	N	P	H	D	O	R	I	C	L	H	O	C	O	N
O	M	E	I	A	E	B	T	O	L	I	V	E	L	T	D
U	E	N	A	N	S	H	A	D	E	S	T	O	E	U	E
R	S	W	H	T	R	A	G	E	D	I	E	S	S	S	R
F	E	R	T	I	L	E	S	B	R	A	Z	I	E	R	S
C	O	I	N	S	M	A	R	B	L	E	H	O	N	E	Y

The Parthenon temple on the Acropolis ("high city")

1. **H E** R **O** D **O** T **U S** The "father of history."
2. ___ ___ R ___ ___ L ___ ___ Was a great Athenian.
3. ___ R ___ R ___ ___ ___ S Were Greek warships.
4. H ___ ___ L ___ ___ Was Ancient Greece.
5. ___ ___ ___ Y ___ P ___ ___ Held the ancient Games.
6. S ___ ___ A ___ ___ ___ Was a sea battle.
7. ___ P ___ ___ T ___ A Rival to Athens.
8. ___ M ___ ___ A The last Greek letter.
9. ___ T T ___ ___ ___ ___ Athens and surrounding area.
10. ___ L ___ ___ E Its oil was important.
11. ___ A D ___ ___ God, also known as Pluto.
12. ___ R ___ Z ___ ___ R ___ Heated Greek homes.
13. ___ R ___ ___ ___ N Imported from Egypt.
14. ___ ___ N E ___ Used to sweeten food.
15. ___ ___ R T ___ ___ E Describes rich, crop-growing coastal land.
16. ___ O ___ E ___ First used in ca 600 B.C.
17. ___ ___ N ___ N Used for sails.
18. ___ O ___ ___ S Homer's were taught in schools.
19. ___ O R ___ ___ ___ S E Its shell is made into lyres.
20. ___ O O ___ Women used it to weave cloth.
21. ___ T H ___ ___ S Produced the best pottery.

22. ___ R ___ N ___ ___ Made from tin and copper.
23. ___ ___ R ___ L Used in temple construction.
24. ___ R M ___ ___ ___ Body protection worn by soldiers.
25. ___ H ___ ___ ___ S A powerful Greek city-state.
26. P ___ ___ R ___ S A huge lighthouse.
27. ___ ___ R ___ C Style of temple column.
28. ___ ___ ___ R S ___ ___ O L ___ ___ The Persian capital.
29. ___ E ___ ___ Leader of the Greek gods.
30. ___ ___ R ___ T ___ ___ They attacked Greek merchant ships.
31. ___ L ___ G ___ ___ Broke out in Athens in 429 B.C.
32. L ___ ___ ___ ___ N D ___ ___ ___ A great Spartan general.
33. ___ I ___ G ___ These towers were used in war.
34. ___ H ___ L ___ ___ Father of Alexander the Great.
35. ___ L ___ ___ H ___ ___ ___ A Persian one was used as a war weapon.
36. ___ ___ C H ___ ___ E ___ ___ S A brilliant Greek scientist.
37. T ___ ___ G ___ ___ I ___ S Plays—often about Greek gods and heroes.
38. ___ ___ S ___ S Worn by Greek actors.
39. R ___ ___ ___ L ___ S Children's toys.
40. ___ ___ S ___ ___ Sailed in "Argo."

Ancient Greece

ANSWERS (1)

Page 7
The Early Greeks

1.

2. because of the mountainous terrain
3. They overran the Mycenaean kingdoms but they couldn't read or write
4. Athens and Sparta
5. 1150 B.C.
6. 150 km
7. on Crete
8. wealthy

Page 9
Time Line

1. 404 B.C.
2. 146 B.C.
3. Thebes
4. 450 years
5. Persians
6. Philip II
7. The Dorians
8. one
9. Olympia
10. Answers may vary – to protect their fleet from attacks by land

Page 13
Language

2. the first two letters of the Greek alphabet
3. (a) dead (b) lamb (c) bread (d) boxer (e) thanks (f) trap
4. Teacher check
5. K, O
6. E, T, M

Page 13
Government

1. Pericles
2. Teacher Check
3. Teacher Check
4. Teacher Check

Page 15
Government

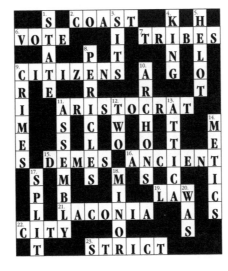

Page 19
Life In Ancient Greece

2. rugs, pottery, fruit, cloth
3. Children playing/men talking
4. Sparta
5. Answers may vary. Current affairs/philosophy
6. Answers may vary
7. water
8. Pluto

Pages 21&23
Homes

1. smoke-filled rooms
2. klismos
3. throne
4. in the gynaikon
5. because the streets were smelly
6. reclining on couches
7. they hadn't been invented
8. Answers may vary – no rubbish collection
9. stone and marble
10. slave gangs

Page 25
Food (1)

(1) mountains (2) infertile
(3) olive (4) lower (5) soil
(6) grain (7) grow (8) feed
(9) quantities (10) imported
(11) India (12) Sicily (13) several
(14) Cyprus (15) valuable (16) life
(17) fresh (18) salted (19) storms
(20) fleets

Page 29
Food (3)

(1) bread (2) cheese (3) chicken
(4) dates (5) eggs (6) fish
(7) honey (8) mushrooms
(9) olives (10) peas (11) pork
(12) porridge

Page 21
Food (31)

ANSWERS (2)

Page 33
Farming (1)
1. olives
2. 6000 B.C.
3. Corinth
4. it was used for cooking and lighting
5. false
6. by hand or dislodged with sticks
7. bread
8. freemen
9. they could grow in poor soil
10. Athens

Page 37
Trade (1)
1. (1) colonies (2) coasts/shores
   (3) difficult (4) roads (5) robber
   (6) attacked (7) cargoes/goods
   (8) imports (9) sails (10) bronze
   (11) slaves (12) Greek (13) work
   (14) homes (15) land

Page 39
Trade (2)
1. metics
2. Egypt and India
3. 600 B.C.
4. kerkouroi
5. Marseilles
6. robbers
7. they were bigger
8. summer
9. Cyprus
10. barter

Page 41
Education
1. Answers may vary

Page 43
Health
(1) give (2) medicine (3) asked
(4) counsel (5) houses (6) go
(7) benefit (8) abstain (9) act
(10) corruption (11) females
(12) slaves (13) professional
(14) connection (15) hear
(16) men (17) divulge (18) all (19) secret

Page 49
Arts and Crafts (2)
1. 3, 2, 5, 1, 4

Page 55
Arts and Crafts (5)

Page 57
The Olympic Games (1)
1. 204
2. true
3. in times of war
4. one race
5. because of corruption
6. Zeus
7. an olympiad
8. The French valued academic studies over sport

Page 63
Gods and Goddesses (1)
2.

Human-like	Not Human-like
married	could control a person's fate
had children	ate special food
quarrelled	could provide special favors
felt jealousy and anger	immortal

Page 67
Athens and Sparta
1. oligarchy
2. Sparta
3. Answers may vary – spoke same language/ worshipped same gods
4. "the same old problem"
5. Answers may vary

Page 69
Peloponnesian Wars
1. (a) Sparta declared war on Athens
   (b) Plague brought in by the Athenian grain ships broke out
   (c) Athens made a foolish attack on Sicily
   (d) the war ended

Page 71
At War
1. Mountain terrain was not suitable for chariots
2. hoplites
3. ephebes
4. Answers may vary – Pegasus
5. Answers may vary

Page 73
Weapons
(1) invented (2) warship (3) oarsmen
(4) archers (5) enemy (6) metal
(7) cripple (8) ships (9) break
(10) unable (11) sail (12) sea
(13) lowered (14) shore (15) battle

Page 75
The Persian Wars (1)

Ancient Greece

ANSWERS (3)

Page 77
The Persian Wars (2)

1. Cyrus
2. They had to pay Persian taxes and serve in the army.
3. The mainland Greeks returned home
4. Marathon
5. Darius I
6. Mainland Greeks assisting colonies and killing his ambassadors
7. three
8. He founded the Persian Empire.
9. They left a track poorly guarded
10. Answers may vary

Page 79
Alexander the Great (1)

Page 81
Alexander The Great (2)

Page 83
The Roman Threat

1. 197 B.C.
2. legionaries
3. He had signed a peace treaty with Hannibal
4. Antiochus III
5. Pydna
6. they became slaves
7. Hannibal
8. twenty-three
9. Lucius Scipio
10. SW

Page 85
Technology

1. (1) brilliant (2) Greece
   (3) evidence (4) pump (5) higher
   (6) invented (7) mounted (8) river
   (9) end (10) water (11) turned
   (12) handle (13) section (14) used
   (15) century
2. (1) scientist (2) invention
   (3) forerunner (4) engine
   (5) sphere (6) mounted (7) boiler
   (8) heated (9) poured (10) spouts
   (11) principle (12) lawn (13) toy
   (14) friends (15) provide
3. (1) crane (2) windlass (3) engineer
   (4) lengths (5) braced (6) spread
   (7) ropes (8) used (9) heavy
   (10) marble (11) temples
   (12) sideways (13) base (14) blocks
   (15) position

Page 89
Entertainment–Theater

1. tragedies, comedies and satires
2. Answers may vary

Page 93
Great Men of the Classical Age (500–300 B.C.)

1. (1) thinkers (2) writings
   (3) students (4) evidence
   (5) questioning (6) power
   (7) influencing (8) tried (9) exile
   (10) drinking
2. (1) influential (2) biology
   (3) reference (4) plants
   (5) ridiculed (6) zoologists
   (7) tutor (8) spread (9) student
   (10) learning
3. (1) leader (2) elected (3) Persians
   (4) power (5) ordinary (6) Athens
   (7) organized (8) public (9) plague
   (10) Sparta

Page 95
In The News!

1. replica
2. comedy
3. Answers may vary
4. a decorative band on a wall
5. as a tourist attraction
6. Aegean Sea
7. Lord Elgin
8. neglected
9. the Arabs
10. lighthouse

Page 98
Legends (1)

1. (1) driven (2) brother
   (3) smuggled (4) claims (5) throne
   (6) Fleece (7) guarded (8) ship
   (9) sail (10) seas (11) fogs
   (12) palace (13) falls (14) return
   (15) obtain (16) dragon
   (17) plotting (18) discover
   (19) murdered (20) leaves
2. (a) Argonauts
   (b) (i) dense (ii) plotting
   (c) Answers may vary e.g., Pelias might kill him
   (d) wanted to be Jason's wife in Greece
   (e) she drugged the dragon
   (f) because of fogs/storms
   (g) Pelias and the King of Colchis
   (h) false
   (i) Answers vary

ANSWERS (4)

Page 99

Legends (2)

(1) fought (2) ruler (3) kidnapped
(4) ruled (5) Achilles (6) warriors
(7) thousand (8) besieged
(9) defended (10) heroes
(11) success (12) horse (13) gift
(14) pretended (15) celebrated
(16) hiding (17) gates
(18) returned (19) husband
(20) rest

Page 101

Eratosthenes

1.

1	2	3	4	5	6	7	8	9	10
11	12	13	14	15	16	17	18	19	20
21	22	23	24	25	26	27	28	29	30
31	32	33	34	35	36	37	38	39	40
41	42	43	44	45	46	47	48	49	50
51	52	53	54	55	56	57	58	59	60
61	62	63	64	65	66	67	68	69	70
71	72	73	74	75	76	77	78	79	80
81	82	83	84	85	86	87	88	89	90
91	92	93	94	95	96	97	98	99	100

2. Answers may vary – the numbers are filtered out
3. 1 is not a prime number – it only has one factor.
4. Answers may vary – e.g. 3 and 5, 17 and 19

Page 102–103

Language

1. metropolis
2. democracy
3. athlete
4. scene
5. draconian
6. throne
7. idiots
8. anchor
9. Olympiad
10. Bible
11. microscopic
12. domestic
13. atlas
14. hector
15. laconic
16. stentorian
17. critics
18. tantalize
19. thespian
20. Hades
21. stadium
22. decathalon
23. planet
24. hypocrite
25. xenophobia

Page 104

Seven Wonders Of The Ancient World

1. Answers will vary
2. The hanging gardens of Babylon.

Page 105

Ancient Greeks–Review 1

(1) c (2) b (3) a (4) b (5) b (6) a
(7) b (8) c (9) c (10) b (11) a (12) c
(13) b (14) c (15) b (16) c (17) c
(18) a (19) b (20) a

Page 106

Ancient Greeks–Review 2

(21) c (22) b (23) a (24) c (25) b
(26) c (27) b (28) c (29) b (30) c
(31) b (32) c (33) b (34) a (35) c
(36) b (37) b (38) a (39) b (40) c

Page 107

Review Word Search

Ancient Greece